# KAREL ++

A Gentle Introduction to the Art
of Object-Oriented Programming

# KAREL ++

## A Gentle Introduction to the Art
## of Object-Oriented Programming

Joseph Bergin

Mark Stehlik

Jim Roberts

Richard Pattis

John Wiley and Sons, Inc.

New York • Chichester • Brisbane • Toronto • Singapore • Weinheim

| ACQUISITIONS EDITOR | Regina Brooks |
| MARKETING MANAGER | Jay Kirsch |
| PRODUCTION EDITOR | Ken Santor |
| DESIGNER | Ann Marie Renzi |
| MANUFACTURING MANAGER | Mark Cirillo |
| ILLUSTRATION | Sigmund Malinowski |
| COVER DESIGN | Nancy Field |
| COVER ART | Image Bank / Michael Shumate |

This book was set in 10/12 Times Roman by Publication Services, Inc., and printed and bound by Courier-Westford, Inc. The cover was printed by Phoenix Color Corp., Inc.

Recognizing the importance of preserving what has been written, it is a
policy of John Wiley & Sons, Inc. to have books of enduring value published
in the United States printed on acid-free paper, and we exert our best
efforts to that end.

The paper on this book was manufactured by a mill whose forest management programs include sustained yield harvesting of its timberlands. Sustained yield harvesting principles ensure that the number of trees cut each year does not exceed the amount of new growth.

Library of Congress Cataloging-in-Publication Data

Karel ++ : a gentle introduction to the art of object-oriented
    programming / Joseph Bergin ... [et al.].
        p.   cm.
    Includes bibliographical references.
    ISBN 0-471-13809-6 (paper : alk. paper)
    1. Object-oriented programming (Computer science)   2. C++
    (Computer program language)   I. Bergin, Joseph.
QA76.64.K37   1997                                    96-35741
629.8'92'01135133–dc20                                CIP

Printed in the United States of America

10 9 8 7 6 5 4 3 2 1

This book is dedicated to our families and to our students.

# PREFACE

The programming landscape has changed significantly since the initial publication of *Karel the Robot* in 1981. Today there are new programming languages, new programming **paradigms**, and new and more powerful computers. Pascal no longer enjoys the popularity it did in the 1980s. However, the concepts of Karel are still as vibrant and valid an introduction to the programming and problem-solving processes as they were when first introduced. However, the object-oriented programming paradigm has begun to dominate the world of commercial software production.

*Karel++* updates *Karel the Robot* to provide a means of introducing novice programmers to object-oriented programming (OOP). This book maintains the simplicity of the original and yet provides instruction that is thoroughly object-oriented from the beginning. Where the original used a syntax and methodology derived from Pascal, the present text is based closely on C++ and Java. In object-oriented programming, a computation is carried out by a set of interacting objects. Here, the objects are robots that exist in a simple world. There can be one or several robots assigned to a task. The programming task is divided into two parts. The first part is defining the capabilities of the robots that are needed. The second is providing a description of the task for the robots to perform. The programmer uses his or her problem solving skills on both parts of this task.

We believe that most people will not actually have to program a computer as part of their everyday lives, either now or in the future. However, many people will need to be able to use a computer and will occasionally need to do something with the machine beyond the "ordinary." Simply put, they will have to solve some type of computer problem. We solve various kinds of problems every day; problem solving is part of our lives. This book will introduce you to problem-solving approaches that can be used with computers. Unfortunately, some people believe programming requires a "different" way of thinking. We don't agree with this statement. Instead of changing the way you think, this book will change how you apply your problem-solving skills to different kinds of problems.

The original *Karel the Robot* used procedures as the fundamental problem solving medium, as is appropriate in procedural programming. Here we apply our problem solving skills, instead, to the design of classes that describe objects (robots), as classes are the primary means of breaking a complex problem into manageable parts in object-oriented programming. The skills of procedural programming and object-oriented programming are very similar, though we look at problems from a slightly different perspective when using OOP.

For the experienced student programmer, this edition should provide insights into the problem-solving and program design processes that will make the student an even better programmer. It will also improve understanding of computer science concepts such as loop invariants and recursion. For individuals who want to begin a thorough sequence of training and education in programming, computer science, or both, *Karel++* provides a solid foundation on which to begin your work.

For novice programmers, this book will give some insight into the programming process from two distinctly different points of view: the planner's and the implementer's. All the problems can be thought about, discussed, and planned in English. Once you have developed your plan, the actual syntax of the robot programming language has very few rules to get in your way as you become the implementer or programmer.

For individuals who do not want to program but need to have a feel for the process, *Karel++* is an excellent tool for providing that insight.

## SUPPLEMENTS

An Instructor's Manual is available for the text that contains numerous pedagogical suggestions for teaching the material based on many years of using *Karel the Robot* in introductory programming courses at the college level; and solutions to most of the in-text exercises.

Software to simulate *Karel++* is available from John Wiley & Sons (accompanying copies of this book).

## ACKNOWLEDGMENTS

As the principal author of this text I most gratefully acknowledge my co-authors and predecessors in this endeavor. First, Richard Pattis is the creator of *Karel the Robot*, which many of us used for many years to introduce Pascal and procedural programming. Jim Roberts and Mark Stehlik, who did the second edition, must also be thanked profusely for improving on an incredibly high standard set by Rich. *Karel++* has been closely based on the second edition of *Karel the Robot*. Although I did the bulk of the editing and designed most of the changes, Rich was always there to force me to keep it simple, and Jim and Mark to make suggestions about what wasn't working. If this work retains any hint of the elegance of the original, it is largely due to their work.

Special thanks to Steven Elliot of Wiley who asked me to do this project. His early support was invaluable. Regina Brooks, our current editor, carried the ball in fine style when Steve had to hand it off. Ken Santor served as the intermediary with Publication Services in the physical preparation of the work. It has been a pleasure working with all of them. Thanks for your constant help. As a group we also want to thank the reviewers of the early manuscripts who kept us on track and suggested many improvements:

Julie Ellis
University of Southern Maine

Walter C. Daugherity
Texas A&M University

Roland Untch
Middle Tennessee State University

Owen Astrachan
Duke University

Jim Polzin
Normandale Community College

Tim Thurman
University of Kansas

Joseph Kmoch
Washington High School

Claire Bono
University of Southern
California—University Park

Barbara Boucher Owens
St. Edward's University

We also want to thank Adrian M. Iley and Josh P. deCesare, students (recently graduated) of Carnegie-Mellon University for creating the software that accompanies this work. We wish them all success in their future careers.

July 1996                                                    Joseph Bergin

# CONTENTS

## Chapter 6   Advanced Techniques for Robots   147

## Appendix A   Robot Programming Summary   177

## Appendix B   Differences Between Karel++ and C++   181

## Appendix C   Differences Between Karel++ and Java   183

# 1  THE ROBOT WORLD

This chapter introduces a class of robots and sketches the world they inhabit. In later chapters, where a greater depth of understanding is necessary, we will amplify this preliminary discussion.

## 1.1  THE ROBOT WORLD

Robots live in a world that is unexciting by today's standards (there are no volcanoes, Chinese restaurants, or symphony orchestras), but it does include enough variety to allow robots to perform simply stated, yet interesting tasks. Informally, the world is a grid of streets that robots can traverse. It also contains special objects that a robot can sense and manipulate.

Figure 1-1 is a map illustrating the structure of the robot world, whose shape is a great flat plane with the standard north, south, east, and west compass points. The world is bounded on its west side by an infinitely long vertical wall extending northward. To the south, the world is bounded by an infinitely long horizontal wall extending eastward. These boundary walls are made of solid neutronium, an impenetrable metal that restrains robots from falling over the edges of the world.

Crisscrossing the world are horizontal streets (running east–west) and vertical avenues (running north–south) at regular, one-block intervals. To help you distinguish between streets and avenues, remember that the *A* in "Avenue" points north and the *V* points south. A corner, sometimes called a <u>street corner</u> or <u>intersection</u>, is located wherever a street and an avenue intersect.

One or more robots can occupy any corner, facing any of the four major compass directions. Any number of robots may occupy the same corner, because the streets and avenues are quite wide. We will usually work with only one robot at a time, however. Robots have names so that we can give them instructions individually. When we work with a single robot we will often call it Karel,[1] though you are free to name the robots that you create with any names you like.

---

[1] The name Karel is used in recognition of the Czechoslovakian dramatist Karel Čapek, who popularized the word *robot* in his play *R.U.R.* (Rossum's Universal Robots). The word *robot* is derived from the Czech word *robota,* meaning "forced labor."

**1**

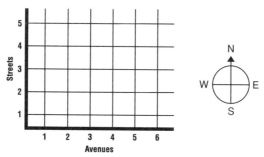

**Figure 1-1**   The Robot World

Both streets and avenues have numbers; consequently, each corner is identified uniquely by its street and avenue numbers. The corner where 1st Street and 1st Avenue intersect is named the <u>origin</u>. The positions of robots and other objects in this world can be described using both <u>absolute</u> and <u>relative</u> locations. The absolute location of the origin, for example, is the intersection of 1st Street and 1st Avenue. An example of a relative location would be to say that a robot is two blocks east and three blocks north of some object in the world. The origin also has a relative location; it is the most southwesterly corner in the robot world. Sometimes we will describe a robot task using language that gives a different interpretation to the robot world, with north as *up,* south *down,* and west and east being *left* and *right,* respectively. This is how we (in the Northern Hemisphere) normally look at maps, of course.

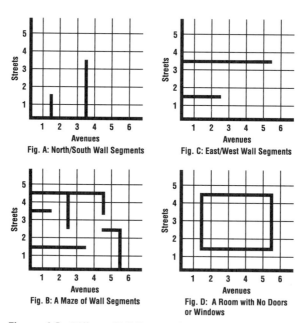

**Figure 1-2**   Different Wall Segment Arrangements in the Robot World

Besides robots, two other kinds of things can occupy this world. The first of these kinds of things is a <u>wall section</u>. Wall sections are also fabricated from the impenetrable metal neutronium, and they can be manufactured in any desired length and pattern. They are positioned between adjacent street corners, effectively blocking a robot's direct path from one corner to the next. Wall sections are used to represent obstacles, such as hurdles and mountains, around which robots must navigate. Enclosed rooms, mazes, and other barriers can also be constructed from wall sections. Figure 1-2 shows some typical wall arrangements a robot might find in the world.

The second kind of thing in the world is a <u>beeper</u>. Beepers are small plastic cones that emit a quiet beeping noise. They are situated on street corners and can be picked up, carried, and put down by robots. Some tasks require one or more robots to pick up or put down patterns made from beepers or to find and transport beepers. Figure 1-3 shows one possible pattern of beepers. Beepers are small so there can be several on a corner, and they don't interfere with robot movement.

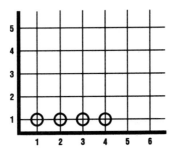

**Figure 1-3**   One Pattern of Beepers in the Robot World

## 1.2   ROBOT CAPABILITIES

Let's now shift our attention away from the robot world and concentrate on the robots themselves. Robots are mobile; a robot can move forward (in the direction it is facing), and it can turn in place. Robots can also perceive their immediate surroundings using rudimentary senses of sight, sound, direction, and touch.

A robot sees by using its TV camera, which points straight ahead. This camera is focused to detect a wall exactly one-half block away from the robot. A robot also has the ability to hear a beeper, but only if the robot and the beeper are on the same corner; the beepers beep very quietly. By consulting its internal compass, a robot can determine which direction it is facing. Finally, each robot is equipped with a mechanical arm that it can use to pick up and put down beepers. To carry these beepers, each robot wears a soundproof <u>beeper-bag</u> around its waist. A robot can also determine whether it is carrying any beepers in this bag by probing the bag with its arm. A robot can also use its arm to determine whether there are other robots on the same corner that it occupies. Finally, a robot can turn itself off when its task is complete.

As you might expect, robots are made in factories. All robots come from the main factory, Karel-Werke, which can actually supply several different models of robots. When we need a robot for a task, we can use the standard model, or we can write a specification for a new model. Karel-Werke is able to build specialized robots that are modifications or extensions of the existing models.

Whenever we want a collection of robots to accomplish a task in the robot world, we must supply a detailed set of instructions that describe any special features of the robots that are needed and also explain how to perform the task. For most tasks one robot is all that is needed. When a robot is ordered from the factory, it is delivered to the robot world by helicopter. The helicopter pilot sets up the robots according to our specifications and reads each new robot a set of instructions to detail its task, which it is then able to carry out.

What language do we use to program (here we use "program" to mean "write instructions for") robots? Instead of programming these robots in English, a natural language for us, we program them in a special <u>programming language</u>. This language was specially designed to be useful for writing robot programs. The robot programming language—like any natural language—has a vocabulary, punctuation marks, and rules of grammar, but this language, unlike English, for example, is simple enough for robots to understand. However, it is a powerful and concise language that allows us to write brief and unambiguous programs for them.

## 1.3 TASKS AND SITUATIONS

A **task** is something that we want a robot to do. The following examples are tasks for robots:

- Move to the corner of 15th St. & 10th Ave.
- Run a hurdle race (with wall sections representing hurdles).
- Escape from an enclosed room that has a door.
- Find a beeper and deposit it on the origin.
- Escape from a maze.

A **situation** is an exact description of what the world looks like. Besides the basic structure of the world, which is always present, wall sections and beepers can be added. To specify a situation completely, we must provide answers for the following questions.

- What is each robot's current position? We must specify both the robot's location (which corner it is on) and what direction it is facing.
- What is the location and length of each wall section in the world?
- What is the location of each beeper in the world? This information includes specifying the number of beepers in each robot's beeper-bag.

Situations are specified in this book by a small map or brief written description. If we know the number of beepers that each robot has in its beeper-bag, then the maps in

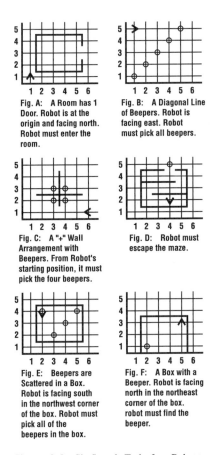

Fig. A:   A Room has 1
Door. Robot is at the
origin and facing north.
Robot must enter the
room.

Fig. B:   A Diagonal Line
of Beepers. Robot is
facing east. Robot
must pick all beepers.

Fig. C:   A "+" Wall
Arrangement with
Beepers. From Robot's
starting position, it must
pick the four beepers.

Fig. D:   Robot must
escape the maze.

Fig. E:   Beepers are
Scattered in a Box.
Robot is facing south
in the northwest corner
of the box. Robot must
pick all of the
beepers in the box.

Fig. F:   A Box with a
Beeper. Robot is facing
north in the northeast
corner of the box.
robot must find the
beeper.

**Figure 1-4**   Six Sample Tasks for a Robot to
Perform

Figure 1-4 completely specify different situations. The <u>initial situation</u> for any task is
defined to be the situation in which all of the robots are placed at the start of the task.
The <u>final situation</u> is the situation that each robot is in when it turns itself off.

Figure 1-4 shows six initial situations that are typical for tasks that a single robot
will accomplish in the coming chapters.

## 1.4   PROBLEM SET

The purpose of this problem set is to make sure that you have a good understanding of
the robot world and the capabilities of robots before moving on to robot programming.

**1.**   Which of the following directions can a robot face?

northeast

east

south-southwest
north
164°
vertical
down

2. What objects other than robots can be found in the robot world?

3. Which of the objects listed in Problem 2 can a robot manipulate or change?

4. What reference points can be used in the robot world to describe a robot's exact location?

5. How many robots can we have in a given robot world?

6. Give the absolute location of each robot in each of the worlds shown in Figure 1-5. Give a relative location of each robot in the worlds.

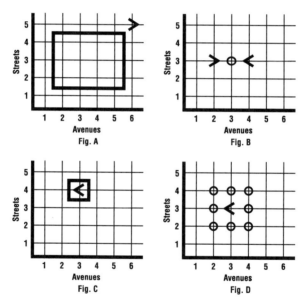

**Figure 1-5**   Different Robot Situations

# 2 PRIMITIVE INSTRUCTIONS AND SIMPLE PROGRAMS

This chapter begins our study of the robot programming language. We will start with a detailed explanation of the primitive instructions that are built into every robot's vocabulary. Using these instructions, we can instruct any robot to move through the world and handle beepers. Section 2.6 shows a complete robot program and discusses the elementary punctuation and grammar rules of the robot programming language. By the end of this chapter we will be able to write programs that instruct robots to perform simple obstacle avoidance and beeper transportation tasks.

Before explaining the primitive instructions of the robot programming language, we must first define the technical term *execute:* A robot executes an instruction by performing the instruction's associated action or actions. The robot executes a program by executing a sequence of instructions that are given to it by the helicopter pilot. Each instruction in such a sequence is delivered to the robot in a message, which directs one robot to perform one instruction in the program.

## 2.1 CHANGING POSITION

Every robot understands two primitive instructions that change its position. The first of these instructions is **move**, which changes a robot's location.

> **move**   When a robot executes a **move** instruction, it moves forward one block; it continues to face the same direction. To avoid damage, a robot will not move forward if it sees a wall section or boundary wall between its current location and the corner to which it would move. Instead, it turns itself off. This action, called an *error shutoff,* will be explained further in Section 2.7.

From this definition we see that a robot executes a **move** instruction by moving forward to the next corner. However, the robot performs an error shutoff when its front is blocked. Both situations are illustrated in Figure 2-1. Figure 2-1 shows the successful execution of a **move** instruction. The wall section is more than one half-block away and cannot block this robot's move.

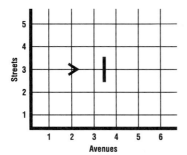

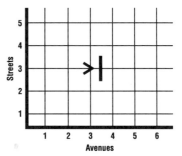

**Figure 2-1 A**    A Robot in the Initial Situation Before a **move** Instruction

**Figure 2-1 B**    A Robot in the Final Situation After Executing a **move** Instruction

In contrast, Figure 2-2 shows an incorrect attempt to move. When this robot tries to execute a **move** instruction in this situation, it sees a wall section. Relying on its self-preservation instinct, it performs an error shutoff.

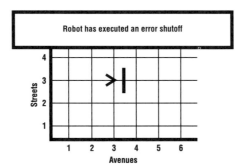

**Figure 2-2**    The Result of a Robot Attempting to **move** When Its Front Is Blocked In an Error Shutoff

## 2.2    TURNING IN PLACE

The second primitive instruction that changes a robot's position is **turnLeft**. This instruction changes the direction in which the robot is facing but does not alter its location.

**turnLeft**    A robot executes a **turnLeft** instruction by pivoting 90° to the left. The robot remains on the same street corner while executing a **turnLeft** instruction. Because it is impossible for a wall section to block a robot's turn, **turnLeft** cannot cause an error shutoff.

A robot always starts a task on some corner, facing either north, south, east, or west. A robot cannot travel fractions of a block or turn at other than 90° angles. Although

**move** and **turnLeft** change the robot's position, after executing either of these instructions, the robot still is on some corner and still is facing one of the four compass directions.

Karel-Werke's designer purposely did not provide a built-in **turnRight** instruction. Would adding a **turnRight** to the primitive instructions allow the robot to perform any task it cannot accomplish without one? A moment's thought—and the right flash of insight—shows that the **turnRight** instruction is unnecessary; it does not permit robots to accomplish any new tasks. The key observation for verifying this conclusion is that a robot can manage the equivalent of a **turnRight** instruction by executing three **turnLeft** instructions.

## 2.3   FINISHING A TASK

We need a way to tell a robot that its task is finished. The **turnOff** instruction fulfills this requirement.

turnOff   When a robot executes a **turnOff** instruction, it turns off and is incapable of executing any more instructions until restarted on another task. The last instruction executed by every robot in a program must be a **turnOff** instruction.

## 2.4   HANDLING BEEPERS

Every robot understands two instructions that permit it to handle beepers. These two instructions perform opposite actions.

pickBeeper   When a robot executes a **pickBeeper** instruction, it picks up a beeper from the corner on which it is standing and then deposits the beeper in its beeper-bag. If a **pickBeeper** instruction is attempted on a beeperless corner, the robot performs an error shutoff. On a corner with more than one beeper the robot picks up one, and only one, of the beepers and then places it in the beeper-bag.

putBeeper   A robot executes a **putBeeper** instruction by extracting a beeper from its beeper-bag and placing the beeper on the current street corner. If a robot tries to execute a **putBeeper** instruction with an empty beeper-bag, the robot performs an error shutoff. If the robot has more than one beeper in its beeper-bag, it extracts one, and only one, beeper and places it on the current corner.

Beepers are so small that robots can move right by them; only wall sections and boundary walls can block a robot's movement. Robots are also very adept at avoiding each other if two or more show up on the same corner simultaneously.

## 2.5  ROBOT DESCRIPTIONS

All robots produced by Karel-Werke have at least the capabilities just described. As we will see, such robots are very primitive, and we might like robots with additional abilities. Therefore, we must have some way to describe those extra abilities so that the factory can build a robot to our specifications. Karel-Werke employs a simple robot programming language to describe both robot abilities and the lists of robot instructions, called *programs*. The simple model of robot described above is called the **ur_Robot**[1] class. The specification of the **ur_Robot** class in the robot programming language follows.

```
class ur_Robot
{
        void move();
        void turnOff();
        void turnLeft();
        void pickBeeper();
        void putBeeper();
};
```

Following the model class name is a list of <u>instructions</u> for this kind of robot. The list is always written in braces { and }, and the final brace is always followed by a semicolon. Each entry is also terminated by a semicolon.

The five instructions, **move** through **putBeeper**, name actions that **ur_Robots** can perform. We defined each of these actions in the foregoing sections, and we will see many examples of their use throughout this book. The word **void** prefixes each of these instructions to indicate that they return no feedback when executed. Later we will see additional instructions that do produce feedback when executed, rather than changing the state of the robot as these instructions all do. The matching parentheses that follow the instruction names mark them as the names of actions that a robot will be able to carry out.

A sample task for an **ur_Robot** might be to start at the origin, facing east, and then walk three blocks east to a corner known to have a beeper, pick up the beeper, and **turnOff** on that corner. A complete program to accomplish this task is shown next. In this program we name the robot **Karel**, but we could use any convenient name.

```
task
{
        ur_Robot Karel(1, 1, East, 0);
                // Deliver the robot to the origin (1,1),
                // facing East, with no beepers.
        Karel.move();
```

---

[1] *ur* is a German prefix meaning "original" or "primitive." The pronunciation of *ur* is similar to the sound of "oor" in "poor."

```
        Karel.move();
        Karel.move();
        Karel.pickBeeper();
        Karel.turnOff();
};
```

Complete programs will be discussed in the next section.


## 2.6   A COMPLETE PROGRAM

In this section we describe a task for a robot named Karel and a complete program that instructs it to perform the task. The task, illustrated in Figure 2-3, is to transport the beeper from 1st Street and 4th Avenue to 3rd Street and 5th Avenue. After Karel has put down the beeper, it must move one block farther north before turning off.

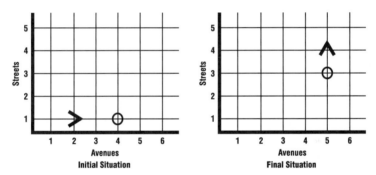

**Figure 2-3**   The Initial and Final Situations of Karel's Task

The following program instructs Karel to perform this task. The program uses all of the instructions available to robots in the **ur_Robot** class, a few new words from the robot programming vocabulary, and punctuation symbols such as the period and semicolon. We will first discuss Karel's execution of this program, and then analyze the general structure of all robot programs.

```
    task
    {
        ur_Robot Karel(1, 2, East, 0);
        Karel.move();
        Karel.move();
        Karel.pickBeeper();
        Karel.move();
        Karel.turnLeft();
        Karel.move();
        Karel.move();
```

```
      Karel.putBeeper();
      Karel.move();
      Karel.turnOff();
  }
```

We must note that this is not the only sequence of instructions that will correctly perform the stated task. Although it is obvious and direct, this is just one of many sequences that will accomplish the task.

A set of instructions for one or more robots is called a *task* and is introduced by the special term, or reserved word, `task`. The first instruction in the main task block constructs the robot, associates the name `Karel` with it, and delivers it from the factory, ready to run, to 1st Street and 2nd Avenue, facing east with no beepers in its beeper-bag. This statement can be thought of as a delivery specification. It instructs the helicopter pilot how to set up the robot when it is delivered. The delivery specification also names the specific type or class of robot that we want delivered. Here we want an `ur_Robot`.

The remaining lines of the main task block instruct Karel how to carry out the task. These instructions are read to Karel by the helicopter pilot, as described next.

## 2.6.1   Executing a Program

Before a program can be executed in a world, the program is read at the factory to make sure it has no errors. We will discuss errors later; for now, we will assume that our program is correct.

How is a program executed? A program execution is begun after the helicopter pilot delivers the robot to the required corner and sets it up according to the delivery specification. Here we require that the `ur_Robot Karel` be set up on 1st Street and 2nd Avenue, facing east, and with zero beepers in its beeper-bag. Then, for each additional command in the main task block, the pilot sends a corresponding electronic message to the robot named in that command. The message gives the instruction that the named robot is supposed to perform. These messages are relayed by the pilot to the robot through a special robot control satellite that hovers over the world. Since a robot can execute only one instruction at a time and since the satellite has a very limited communication capacity, only one instruction can be sent at a time. The pilot must wait for instruction completion before sending the next message. When the robot completes the current instruction, it sends a reply back to the pilot through the satellite indicating that the next instruction can be sent. Messages from the main task block are sent sequentially without omitting any instructions in a strict top-to-bottom order. The pilot continues sending messages until either all messages in the main task block have been sent or the pilot attempts to send a message to a robot that has executed a `turnOff` or has performed an error shutoff.

It is also possible for robots to send messages to each other. When this occurs, the robot sending the message waits for the reply before continuing. This is to guarantee that the satellite communication channel is never overloaded.

To determine what a program does, we <u>simulate</u>, or <u>trace</u>, its execution. Simulating or tracing a robot program means that we must systematically execute the program exactly as the pilot and robots would, recording every action that takes place. We can simulate a robot program by using markers on a sheet of paper (representing robots and the world). We simulate a robot program by following the sequence of instructions in the order the pilot reads them to the robot. We will discuss tracing later, but in order to become proficient robot programmers, we must understand exactly how the pilot reads the program and the robot executes it. The ability to simulate a robot's behavior quickly and accurately is an important skill that we must acquire.

Let's follow a simulation of our program. In the following simulation (1, 4) means 1st Street and 4th Avenue. In the following annotation we explain exactly what state the robot is left in after the execution of the instruction. Note that the symbol / / (two adjacent slash characters) is used in the simulation to introduce <u>comments</u> into our robot programs. Each comment begins with the / / mark and continues to the end of the line. These comments are ignored by the pilot and by the robots; they are included only to aid our own understanding of the program. Here we use them to explain in detail each instruction as it will be executed. We note, however, that if the program is changed in any way, the comments are likely to become invalid.

```
task
{
        ur_Robot Karel(1, 2, East, 0);
                        // A new robot named Karel is
                        // constructed and delivered to
                        // (1, 2), facing East. Karel has
                        // no beepers in its beeper-bag.

        Karel.move();           // Karel moves east
                                // to (1, 3)
        Karel.move();           // Karel moves east
                                // to (1, 4)
        Karel.pickBeeper();     // Karel picks 1 beeper,
                                // 1 beeper in bag
        Karel.move();           // Karel moves east
                                // to (1, 5)
        Karel.turnLeft();       // Karel remains on
                                // (1, 5), faces North
        Karel.move();           // Karel moves north
                                // to (2, 5)
        Karel.move;             // Karel moves north
                                // to (3, 5)
        Karel.putBeeper();      // Karel puts 1 beeper
                                // down, now 0 beepers
                                // in bag
        Karel.move();           // Karel moves north
                                // to (4, 5)
```

```
        Karel.turnOff();        // Karel remains on
                                // (4, 5) facing North
                                // and shuts off
    }
```

Karel is done and we have <u>verified</u> that our program is correct through simulation by tracing the execution of the program.

## 2.6.2   The Form of Robot Programs

Now that we have seen how a robot executes a program, let's explore the grammar rules of the robot programming language. The factory and pilots pay strict attention to grammar and punctuation rules, so our time is well spent carefully studying these rules. We start by dividing the symbols in a robot program into three groups. The first group consists of <u>special symbols</u>. It has members such as the punctuation marks like the semicolon, the braces { and }, and the period. The next group of symbols consists of <u>names</u> such as robot and class names, **Karel** and **ur_Robot**. We also use names to refer to <u>instructions</u>, like **putBeeper** and **turnLeft**. The third and last group of symbols consists of reserved words. We have already seen a few of these like **class** and **task**.

Reserved words are used to structure and organize the primitive instructions in the robot programming language. They are called *reserved* words because their use is reserved for their built-in purpose. These reserved words may not be reused for other purposes in a robot program, such as robot names. To make the reading of programs easier, we may write robot programs using both upper- and lowercase letters as well as the underscore character, but we must be consistent. For example, **task** is always spelled with all lowercase letters. The robot programming language is *case-sensitive,* meaning that the use of upper- and lowercase letters in a word must be consistent each time the word is used. If we use the word **Task** in a robot program it would refer to something else, perhaps the name of a robot.

Since robot programs need to be read by humans as well as robots, it is helpful to be able to put explanatory material into the program itself. The language therefore permits comments to be inserted into the text of the program. As we have seen in the foregoing program, a comment begins anywhere on a line with the special symbol **//** (two slash marks with no space between). The comment terminates only when the line does. Anything may be put on the line following the comment symbol.

Every robot program consists of a single task for one or more robots. This <u>main task block</u> is introduced by the reserved word **task** and is enclosed in curly brace punctuation marks. Notice that the opening brace must be matched eventually by a closing brace. Matching pairs of braces are called <u>delimiters,</u> because they mark, or delimit, the beginning and end of some important entity.

If we needed specialized robots to perform various parts of the task, the class declarations of those robots would precede the task list, as would the definitions of any new instructions named in the class declarations. We will go into this in detail in Chapter 3.

The main task block itself starts with a list of definitions, called <u>declarations</u>. In the following program we have only one declaration, which declares that the name **Karel** will be used as the name of a robot in class **ur_Robot**. Declarations introduce new names and indicate how they will be used in the rest of the program. The declarations of robot names always end with a semicolon. We could also declare names for several different robots, even robots of different classes. The declarations of robots can best be thought of as delivery specifications to the factory. They always contain information about how the robot should be placed in the world.

Every program has one main task block. Each of the statements in the main task block is terminated by a semicolon. Most of the statements in the main task block are instructions to the robots declared in the declaration list. The one exception here is the delivery instruction, which causes the factory to construct and deliver a new **ur_Robot** named Karel to 1st Street and 2nd Avenue (we always list streets first), facing east, with no beepers in its beeper-bag. When delivered, the robot is set up and ready to execute instructions sent to it. Since robots are delivered by the factory in helicopters, we don't need to be concerned about walls in the world that might impede delivery to any corner. The helicopter will be able to fly over them.

Instructions given to a specific robot are called <u>messages</u>. We can send messages to several different robots from the same main task block, so we need to specify which robot is to carry out each instruction. Thus, if we have a robot named Karel and want it to move, we send the <u>message</u> **Karel.move()**. This seems redundant here when there is only one robot, but it is required nevertheless. An instruction that causes a robot to perform one of its own instructions, such as move, is known as a <u>message statement</u>. The instruction named in a message statement (**move**) is called the <u>message</u>, and the robot (**Karel**) is the <u>receiver of the message.</u> Messages are the means of getting a robot to execute an instruction.

Execution always begins with the first instruction following the reserved word **task**. Robots are **not** automatically shut down at the final closing brace in a program; the **turnOff** instruction must be used for that purpose. The closing brace marks the end of the instructions that will be executed. If we reach the end of the instructions in the main task block and any robot is still on because it hasn't yet executed a **turnOff** instruction, it means that at least one **turnOff** instruction has been omitted from the program, and any robot still on will report an error.

Observe that the program is nicely indented as well as commented. It is well organized and easy to read. This style of indenting, as well as the comments, is only for the benefit of human readers. The following program is just as easily executed as the previous program.

```
task { ur_Robot Karel(1,2, East,0); Karel.move();
Karel.move(); Karel.pickBeeper(); Karel.move();
Karel.turnLeft(); Karel.move(); Karel.move();
Karel.putBeeper(); Karel.move(); Karel.turnOff(); }
```

As this example illustrates, the importance of adopting a programming style that is easy to read by humans cannot be overemphasized.

## 2.7  ERROR SHUTOFFS

When a robot is prevented from successfully completing the action associated with an instruction, it turns itself off. This action is known as an error shutoff, and the effect is equivalent to executing a **turnOff** instruction. However, turning off is not the only way such a problem could be addressed. An alternative strategy could have the robot just ignore any instruction that cannot be executed successfully. Using this strategy the robot could continue executing the program as if it had never been required to execute the unsuccessful instruction.

To justify the choice of executing an error shutoff, rather than just ignoring instructions in such situations, consider the following: Once an unexpected situation arises—one that prevents successful execution of an instruction—a robot probably will be unable to make further progress toward accomplishing the task. Continuing to execute a program under these circumstances will lead to an even greater discrepancy between what the programmer had intended for the robot to do and what it is actually doing. Consequently, the best strategy is to have the robot turn off as soon as the first inconsistency appears.

So far, we have seen three instructions that can cause error shutoffs: **move**, **pickBeeper**, and **putBeeper**. We must construct our programs carefully and ensure that the following conditions are always satisfied.

- A robot executes a **move** instruction only when the path is clear to the next corner immediately in front of it.
- A robot executes a **pickBeeper** instruction only when it is on the same corner as at least one beeper.
- A robot executes a **putBeeper** instruction only when the beeper-bag is not empty.
- A robot executes a **turnOff** instruction at the end of each program.

We can guarantee that these conditions are met if, before writing our program, we know the exact initial situation in which the robot will be placed.

## 2.8  PROGRAMMING ERRORS

In this section we classify all programming errors into four broad categories. These categories are discussed using the analogy of a motorist with a task in the real world. It should help clarify the nature of each error type. You might ask, "Why spend so much time talking about errors when they should never occur?" The answer to this question is that programming requires an uncommon amount of precision, and although errors should not occur in principle, they occur excessively in practice. Therefore we must become adept at quickly finding and fixing errors by simulating our programs.

A lexical error occurs whenever the robot program contains a word that is not in its vocabulary. As an analogy, suppose that we are standing on a street in San Francisco and we are asked by a lost motorist, "How can I get to Portland, Oregon?" If we tell the motorist, "fsdt jkhpy hqngrpz fgssj sgr ghhgh grmplhms," we commit a lexical error.

The motorist is unable to follow our instructions because it is impossible to decipher the words of which the instructions are composed. Similarly, the robot executing a program must understand each word in a program that it is asked to execute.

Here is a robot program with some lexical errors:

```
taxt                    // misspelled reserved word
{
  ur_Robot Karel(1,2, East, 0) ;
  Karel.move();
  Karel.mvoe();         // misspelled instruction
  Karel.pick();         // unknown word
  Karel.move();
  Karel.turnright();    // unknown word
  Karel.turnleft();     // unknown word
  Karel.move();
}
```

The last error occurs because the robot programming language is case-sensitive. The word turnLeft is not the same as turnleft.

Even if the pilot recognizes every word in a program, the program still might harbor a <u>syntax error</u>. This type of error occurs whenever we use incorrect grammar or incorrect punctuation. Going back to our lost motorist, we might reply, "for, Keep hundred. just miles going eight." Although the motorist recognizes each of these words individually, we have combined them in a senseless, convoluted manner. According to the rules of English grammar, the parts of speech are not in their correct positions. We discussed the grammar rules for basic robot programs in Section 2.6.2.

The following program contains no lexical errors, but it does have syntax errors.

```
ur_Robot Karel(1,1,East,0); // declaration not in
                            // main task block
task                        // missing brace
  Karel.move();
  move();                   // not addressed
                            // to any robot
  Karel.pickBeeper          // no ()
  Karel :: move();          // incorrect use of ::
  Karel.turnLeft()          // missing semicolon
  Karel.move();
  Karel.move();
  Karel.put-beeper();       // use capitalization,
                            // not dash.
  Karel.move();
};                          // extra semicolon
  Karel.turnOff()           // instruction outside
                            // task block and
                            // missing semicolon
```

If our program contains lexical or syntax errors, the factory will discover them when our program is checked there. In both cases, the factory has no conception of what we *meant* to say; therefore, it does not try to correct our errors. Instead, the factory informs us of the detected errors and doesn't build the robot. This action is not an error shutoff, for in this case the robot never has a chance to begin to execute the program. While discussing the next two categories of errors, we will assume that the factory finds no lexical or syntax errors in our program, so it builds the robot and the pilot delivers it and begins to execute the program.

The third error category is called an execution error. Unlike lexical and syntax errors, which are detected at the factory, the pilot can only detect these errors while the program is running or during a simulation of its execution. Execution errors occur whenever a robot in the world is unable to execute an instruction successfully and is forced to perform an error shutoff. Returning to our motorist, who is trying to drive from San Francisco to Portland, we might say, "Just keep going for eight hundred miles." But if the motorist happens to be facing west at the time, and takes our directions literally, the motorist would reach the Pacific Ocean after traveling only a few miles. At this point, the motorist would halt, realizing that he or she cannot follow our instructions to completion.

Likewise, a robot turns off if asked to execute an instruction that it cannot execute successfully. Instructing a robot to **move** when the front is blocked, to **pickBeeper** on a corner that has no beeper, and to **putBeeper** when the beeper-bag is empty are examples of execution errors, and each one results in an error shutoff.

The final error class is the most insidious, because pilots, the factory, and robots cannot detect this type of error when it occurs. We label this category of error an intent error. An intent error occurs whenever the program successfully terminates but does not successfully complete the task. Suppose our motorist is facing south when we say, "Just keep going for eight hundred miles." Even though these instructions can be successfully followed to completion, the motorist will end up somewhere in Mexico, rather than Oregon.

Here is an example of an intent error in a robot program: Beginning in the situation shown in Figure 2-4, Karel is to pick up the beeper, move it one block to the north, put the beeper down, move one more block to the north, and **turnOff**.

```
task
{ ur_Robot Karel(3,2, East, 0);
  Karel.move();
  Karel.pickBeeper();
  Karel.move();
  Karel.turnLeft();
  Karel.putBeeper();
  Karel.move();
  Karel.turnOff();
}
```

There are no lexical, syntax, or execution errors in this program. As far as Karel and the helicopter pilot are concerned, when the **turnOff** is executed, everything is

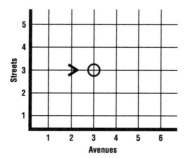

**Figure 2-4** Karel's Initial Situation

perfect. However, look at the task and look at the program. What is the error? The task is to move the beeper one block to the north, yet Karel moved the beeper one block to the east. The intent was a northerly move, but the final result was an easterly move. The program does not satisfy the requirements of the stated task and thus contains an error of intent.

Remember that a robot does not understand the task for which we have programmed it. All that the robot can do is execute the instructions we have sent it in our program. Thus, there is no way for a robot to know that the program did not accomplish what we intended. Similarly, the pilot has no way to know what we intended. He or she only knows what is actually written in the program itself.

## 2.8.1 Bugs and Debugging

In programming jargon, all types of errors are known as <u>bugs</u>. There are many apocryphal stories about the origin of this term. In one story the term *bug* is said to have been originated by telephone company engineers to refer to the source of random noises transmitted by their electronic communications circuits. Another story originated with the Harvard Mark I Computer and Grace Murray Hopper, later Admiral. The computer was producing incorrect answers, and when engineers took it apart trying to locate the problem, they found a dead moth caught between the contacts of a relay, causing the malfunction: the first computer bug. Other stories abound, so perhaps we shall never know the true entomology of this word.

Perhaps the term *bug* became popular in programming because it saved the egos of programmers. Instead of admitting that their programs were full of errors, they could say that their programs had bugs in them. Actually, the metaphor is apt; bugs are hard to find, and although a located bug is frequently easy to fix, it is difficult to ensure that all bugs have been found and removed from a program. <u>Debugging</u> is the name that programmers give to the activity of removing errors from a program.

## 2.9 PROBLEM SET

The purpose of this problem set is to test your knowledge of the form and content of simple robot programs. The programs you are required to write are long but not

complicated. Concentrate on writing grammatically correct, pleasingly styled programs. Refer back to the program and discussion in Section 2.6 for rules and examples
of correct grammar and punctuation. Each of these problems requires a single robot
of the **ur_Robot** class. In each case we assume it will be named Karel. This is not
required, however, and you are, in general, free to name your robots with other names.
Verify that each program is correct by simulating Karel's actions in the appropriate
initial situation.

1.  Start a robot in the initial situation illustrated in Figure 2-5 and simulate the
    execution of the following program. Karel's task is to find the beeper, pick it
    up, and then turn itself off. Draw a map of the final situation, stating whether
    an error occurs. If an execution or intent error does occur, explain how you
    would correct the program. This program has no lexical or syntactic errors.

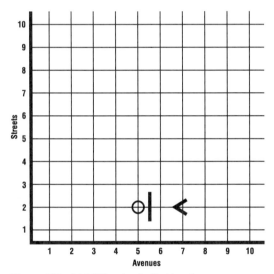

**Figure 2-5**    Initial Situation for Problem 1

```
task
{ ur_Robot Karel(2, 7, West, 0);
  Karel.move();
  Karel.turnLeft();
  Karel.turnLeft();
  Karel.move();
  Karel.turnLeft();
  Karel.move();
  Karel.turnLeft();
  Karel.move();
  Karel.pickBeeper();
  Karel.turnOff();
}
```

2.  Carefully inspect the following program and correct all lexical and syntactic errors. *Hint:* There are nine errors. Four errors involve semicolons, three are syntactical, and one is lexical. (Yes, there is another error too.) Confirm that each word is in an appropriate place and that it is a correctly spelled instruction name or reserved word. You may use the program in Problem 1 as a model for a lexically and syntactically correct program.

```
task
{ ur_Robot Karel(2,7, East, 0);
  Karel.move();
  Karel.move()
  Karel.pickBeeper();
  Karel.move;();
  Karel.turnLeft();
  move();
  Karel.move();
  Karel.turnright;
  Karel.putBeeper();
  Karel.putBeeper();
  Karel.turnOff
};
```

3.  What is the smallest lexically and syntactically correct robot program?

4.  In most cities and towns we can walk around the block by repeating the following actions four times:

    Walk to the nearest intersection
    Turn either right or left (the same one each time)

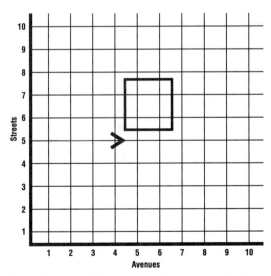

**Figure 2-6**   Initial Situation for the Walk-Around-the-Block Task

If this is done correctly, we will return to our original starting place. Program Karel to walk around the block. Will your program succeed for the initial situation in Figure 2-6?

**5.** Every morning Karel is awakened in bed when the newspaper, represented by a beeper, is thrown on the front porch of the house. Program Karel to retrieve the paper and bring it back to bed. The initial situation is given in Figure 2-7, and the final situation must have Karel back in bed (same corner, same direction) with the newspaper.

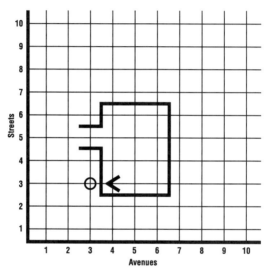

**Figure  2-7**   Initial Situation for the Newspaper Retrieval Task

**6.** The wall sections in Figure 2-8 represent a mountain (north is up). Program Karel to climb the mountain and then plant a flag, represented by a beeper, on the summit; Karel then must descend the other side of the mountain. Assume that Karel starts with the flag-beeper in the beeper-bag. Remember that Karel is not a super-robot that can leap to the top of the mountain, plant the flag, and then jump down in a single bound. As illustrated, Karel must closely follow the mountain's face on the way up and down.

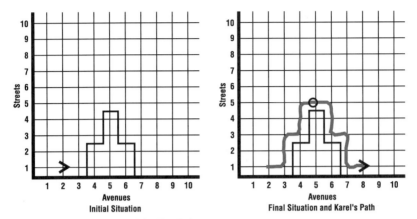

**Figure 2-8** The Mountain Climbing Task

7. On the way home from the supermarket, Karel's shopping bag ripped slightly at the bottom, leaking a few expensive items. These groceries are represented by—you guessed it—beepers. The initial situation, when Karel discovered the leak, is represented in Figure 2-9. Program Karel to pick up all the dropped items and then return to the starting position.

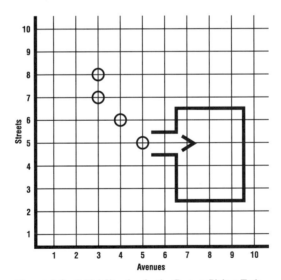

**Figure 2-9** Initial Situation for the Grocery Pickup Task

8.  Write a program that instructs Karel to rearrange the beeper pattern as shown in Figure 2-10.

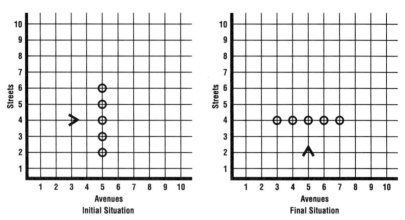

**Figure 2-10**   The Rearrange-the-Beepers Task

9.  Karel is practicing for the Robot Olympics. One of Karel's events is the shuttle race. The shuttle race requires Karel to move around two beepers in a figure 8 pattern as shown in Figure 2-11. Write a program that instructs Karel to walk a figure 8 pattern as fast as possible ("fast" implies as few instructions as possible). Karel must stop in the same place it starts and must be facing the same direction.

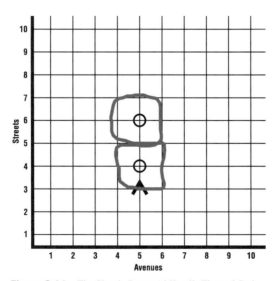

**Figure 2-11**   The Shuttle Race and Karel's Figure 8 Path

# 3 EXTENDING THE ROBOT PROGRAMMING LANGUAGE

This chapter explains the mechanics of specifying new classes of robots and adding new instructions to the robot vocabulary. It also discusses methods for planning, implementing, and testing our programs. The ability to extend the robot vocabulary combined with these techniques can simplify our work in writing robot programs.

## 3.1 CREATING A MORE NATURAL PROGRAMMING LANGUAGE

In Chapter 2, we saw a robot perform a complex task. We also saw that it takes many instructions to perform such a task. Writing so many instructions is verbose and error prone.

Let's look at a particularly clumsy aspect of robot programming. Suppose that we need to program a robot to travel over vast distances. For example, assume that, starting at 3rd Avenue and 2nd Street, the robot must move east along 2nd Street for 10 miles (a mile is eight blocks long), pick up a beeper, and then move another 5 miles north. Because a robot understands about moving *blocks* but not *miles,* we must translate our solution into instructions that move the robot one block at a time. This restriction forces us to write a program that contains 120 move instructions. Although the conversion from miles to blocks is straightforward, it results in a very long and cumbersome program.

The crux of the problem is that we think in one language but must program robots in another. Rather than make programmers the slaves of the machine, continually forced to translate their powerful ideas into the robot's primitive instructions, Karel-Werke turned the tables and endowed robots with a simple mechanism to *learn* the definitions of new instructions.

The robot programming language permits the robot programmer to specify new classes of robots. These class descriptions provide specifications of new robot instructions. Karel-Werke will then use the class descriptions to create robots able to carry out the new instructions.

A robot's learning ability is quite limited. Karel-Werke builds each robot with a dictionary of useful instruction names and their definitions, but each definition must be built from simpler instructions that robots already understand. By providing robots with a dictionary of instructions that perform complex actions, we can build a robot vocabulary that corresponds more closely to our own. Given this mechanism, we can solve our programming problems using whatever instructions are natural to our way of thinking, and then we can provide robots with the definitions of these instructions.

We can define a **moveMile** instruction as eight **move** instructions. Then, when a robot is told to **moveMile** in a program, it looks up the definition associated with this instruction name and executes it. Now our unwieldy beeper-moving program can be written with a **moveMile** definition, containing eight **move** instructions and another 15 **moveMile** instructions. This program, containing these 23 instructions, would be quite an improvement over the original program, which needed more than 120 instructions to accomplish the task.

Although both programs move the robot exactly the same distance, the smaller program is much easier to read and understand. In complicated problems, the ability to extend a robot's vocabulary makes the difference between understandable programs and unintelligible ones. We will explore in detail this extremely important definition mechanism in the next two sections.

## 3.2   A MECHANISM THAT DEFINES NEW CLASSES OF ROBOTS

Back in Chapter 2 we saw the declaration of the primitive **ur_Robot** class. Users of the robot language can also declare new classes of robots and the factory will be able to deliver them, just as it does the standard robots. To specify a new class of robots, we include a class specification in the declaration section at the beginning of our robot program. Isolated from a program, the general form of the specification is shown in the following template.

```
class <new-class-name> :<old-class-name>
{
    <list-of-instructions>
};¹

<definitions-of-the-new-instructions>
```

The class specification uses the reserved word **class** and the special symbols colon and braces to separate the various parts of the declaration. This general form includes elements delimited by angle brackets, < and >, which must be replaced with appropriate substitutions when we include a class specification in a robot program. Angle brackets are not part of the robot programming language; they are just a way to set off locations in a program structure where actual language elements may appear. In this case, <new-class-name> must be replaced by a new name, not yet used in the program. This name can be built from upper-case and lower-case letters, digits, and

---

[1] A few other things can be included in a robot class declaration. These will be introduced in future chapters.

the underscore character but must not match any other name in the program or the spelling of any reserved word. Names must also **begin** with a letter. The replacement for <old-class-name> is the name of an existing robot class, either **ur_Robot** or one previously declared in the same program. New instructions that apply to this class of robot will replace <list-of-instructions>, and we will soon see how to define new instructions, which would replace <definitions-of-the-new-instructions>.

Suppose that we would like to solve the mile mover problem discussed in the introduction to this chapter. Suppose also that, in addition to the new capabilities, we want the robots of the new class to have all of the functionality of the standard **ur_Robot** class. We can do so with a new class specification as follows:

```
class Mile_Walker: ur_Robot
{
        void moveMile();
};
```

The name of the new class of robots is **Mile_Walker**, which also names its main new capability. We also indicate, by giving the name of the **ur_Robot** class following the colon, that mile walkers are to have all of the capabilities of members of the **ur_Robot** class. As a shorthand we say that **ur_Robot** is the parent class of **Mile_Walker** or that **Mile_Walker** is derived from **ur_Robot**. We also say that robots of the new class inherit all the capabilities of the parent class. Therefore mile walkers know how to **move** and **turnLeft**, just like members of the **ur_Robot** class. They can also pick and put beepers and turn themselves off.

Here we have a list of only a single new instruction. Each instruction in the list is terminated by a semicolon. This specification says that when a robot in this class is first turned on it will be able to execute **moveMile** instructions as well as all instructions inherited from the **ur_Robot** class.

We will see later that the names of instructions can be new names or the names of instructions already existing in the parent class. In this latter case we can give new meaning to instructions, as we shall see in Section 3.6.

The class declaration introduces the names of new robot instructions, but it does not explain how they are to be carried out. The next section will show how to define the new capabilities.

## 3.3 DEFINING THE NEW INSTRUCTIONS

Once we have declared a new robot class we need to define all of the new instructions introduced in it. These definitions follow the class declaration in the declaration part of the robot program. The form of an instruction definition is as follows.

```
void <class-name> :: <instruction-name>   ()
{
        <list-of-instructions>
}
```

We begin with the reserved word **void**. We have to give the name of the instruction we are defining, of course. However, since we can define several robot classes, and these classes can actually reuse the same instruction names, we must also give the name of the robot class to which this instruction belongs. The name of the class is separated from the name of the instruction by the scope resolution operator **::**. Between the brace delimiters, we give a list of instructions, similar to a main task block, that tells a robot of this class how to carry out the instruction. This list of instructions delimited by braces is called a <u>block</u> in the robot programming vocabulary. Again, every instruction in the list is terminated by a semicolon. For example, our **moveMile** instruction in the **Mile_Walker** class would be

```
void Mile_Walker :: moveMile()
{
        move();
        move();
        move();
        move();
        move();
        move();
        move();
        move();
}
```

This block is like a main task block, but it is also different, because the instructions in it are not prefaced here with the name of any robot. The reason for the difference is that in the main task block, we need to tell some particular robot to carry out an instruction, so we say something like **Karel.move()** to get a robot named Karel to move. Here, however, a robot of the **Mile_Walker** class will eventually carry out this instruction when it is sent a **moveMile** message. The robot will carry out this instruction list itself. Since it is moving itself and not another robot, a robot's name is not needed here.

The language could have been designed so that robots referred to themselves with a special reserved word such as **myself**, in which case the move instructions in the previous example would be replaced by **myself.move**, but this was not done. It makes the language more concise.

If we have a **Mile_Walker** named Lisa, we can get it to walk a mile with either

```
Lisa.moveMile();
```

or

```
Lisa.move();
Lisa.move();
Lisa.move();
Lisa.move();
Lisa.move();
```

```
Lisa.move();
Lisa.move();
Lisa.move();
```

In the former case, Lisa will **move** itself eight times upon receiving the single
**moveMile** message.

The complete robot program for this is as follows:

```
class Mile_Walker: ur_Robot{
        void moveMile();
};

void Mile_Walker :: moveMile()
{
        move();
        move();
        move();
        move();
        move();
        move();
        move();
        move();
}

task
{    Mile_Walker Lisa(3, 2, East, 0);
        // Declare a new Mile_Walker Lisa.
        Lisa.moveMile();
        Lisa.moveMile();
        Lisa.moveMile();
        Lisa.moveMile();
        Lisa.moveMile();
        Lisa.moveMile();
        Lisa.moveMile();
        Lisa.moveMile();
        Lisa.moveMile();
        Lisa.moveMile();
        Lisa.pickBeeper();
        Lisa.turnLeft();
        Lisa.moveMile();
        Lisa.moveMile();
        Lisa.moveMile();
        Lisa.moveMile();
        Lisa.moveMile();
        Lisa.turnOff();
}
```

Notice that having a **moveFiveMiles** instruction here would be useful. Contemplate writing the program without defining any new instructions. It requires 122 messages to be sent to the robot. This is not hard to write with a good text editor, but once it is written, it is tedious to verify that it has exactly the right number of move commands.

## 3.4   THE MEANING AND CORRECTNESS OF NEW INSTRUCTIONS

A robot is a machine, a device completely devoid of intelligence. This is something that robot programmers must never forget. The robot does not "understand" what we "mean" when we write a program. It does exactly what we "say"—there is no room for interpretation. A robot class declaration is a description to the robot factory that tells it how to construct robots of this class. At the robot factory the entire declaration part of any robot program is read and examined for errors. As part of the manufacturing and delivery process the robots are given the definitions of each of the new instructions of their class. Each robot stores the definitions of the instructions in its own dictionary of instructions. Thus, when we tell a robot of the **Mile_Walker** class to **moveMile**, it receives the message, consults its dictionary to see how it must respond, and then carries out the required actions. The helicopter pilot does not have to read this part of the program when setting up robots for delivery.

In a robot's world, just because we define a new instruction named **moveMile**, it doesn't necessarily mean that the instruction really moves the robot one mile. For example, there is nothing that prevents the use of the following instruction definition:

```
void Mile_Walker :: moveMile()
{
        move();
        move();
        move();
        move();
        move();
        move();
}
```

According to robot programming rules of grammar, this is a perfectly legal definition: It contains neither lexical nor syntax errors. However, by defining **moveMile** this way, we tell a robot that executing a **moveMile** instruction is equivalent to executing six **move** instructions. The robot does not understand what a **moveMile** instruction is supposed to accomplish; its only conception of a **moveMile** instruction is the definition we provide. Consequently, any new instruction we define may contain an intent error, as this example shows.

Besides intent errors, a new instruction can cause execution errors if it is defined by using primitive instructions that can cause error shutoffs. Can this incorrect definition of **moveMile** ever cause an error shutoff? The answer is yes, because we might encounter a wall before we completed six moves. However, it is possible to write a set of instructions for a robot to execute in which it would seem that nothing is wrong with this version of **moveMile**. Thus we might gain false confidence in this incorrect instruction and be very surprised when it fails later. This example is somewhat trivial because the error is obvious. With a more complex defined instruction, we must take care to write a definition that really accomplishes what its name implies. The name specifies what the instruction is intended to do, and the definition specifies how the instruction does what the name implies. The two must match exactly, if we are to understand what our programs mean. If not, one or both must be changed.

When simulating a robot's execution of a defined instruction, we must adhere to the rules that the robot uses to execute these instructions. Robots execute a defined instruction by performing the actions associated with its definition. Do not try to short-cut this process by doing what the instruction *name* means because the robot does not know what a defined instruction means; the robot knows only how it is defined. We must recognize the significance of this distinction and learn to interpret robot programs as literally as the robot does. The meaning of names is supposed to help a human reader understand a program. If the actual instructions defining the meaning of a name are at variance with the meaning of the name, it is easy to be misled.

## 3.5   DEFINING NEW INSTRUCTIONS IN A PROGRAM

In this section we display a complete robot program that uses the instruction definition mechanism. We will first trace the execution of the program (recall that tracing is just simulating the execution of the instructions in the order that a robot does). We will then discuss the general form of programs that use the new instruction definition mechanism. The task is shown in Figure 3-1: It must pick up each beeper in the world while climbing the stairs. The following is a program that correctly instructs a robot to accomplish the task.

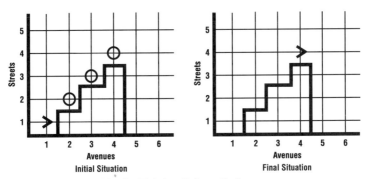

**Figure 3-1**   A Stair-Cleaning Task for a Robot to Perform

```
class Stair_Sweeper: ur_Robot
{
        void climbStair();
        void turnRight();
};
```

```
void Stair_Sweeper :: turnRight()
{
        turnLeft();
        turnLeft();
        turnLeft();
}

void Stair_Sweeper :: climbStair()
{
        turnLeft();
        move();
        turnRight();
        move();
}

task
{       Stair_Sweeper Alex(1, 1, East, 0);

        Alex.climbStair();
        Alex.pickBeeper();
        Alex.climbStair();
        Alex.pickBeeper();
        Alex.climbStair();
        Alex.pickBeeper();
        Alex.turnOff();
}
```

Next we provide an annotated version of the same program that numbers each instruction in the order in which it is executed, starting with the delivery specification instruction #0:

```
class Stair_Sweeper: ur_Robot
{
        void climbStair();
        void turnRight();
};

void Stair_Sweeper :: turnRight()
{
    // to here from #4 or          #13 or          #22
    turnLeft();     #5 or          #14 or          #23
    turnLeft();     #6 or          #15 or          #24
    turnLeft();     #7 or          #16 or          #25
} //   return to    #4  return to #13  return to #22
```

```
void Stair_Sweeper :: climbStair()
{
    // to here from #1 or          #10 or           #19
    turnLeft();      #2            #11              #20
    move();          #3            #12              #21
    turnRight();     #4            #13              #22
    move();          #8            #17              #26
} //     return to  #1  return to #10  return to #19


task
{   Stair_Sweeper Alex(1, 1, East, 0);        #0
    Alex.climbStair();                        #1
    Alex.pickBeeper();                        #9
    Alex.climbStair();                        #10
    Alex.pickBeeper();                        #18
    Alex.climbStair();                        #19
    Alex.pickBeeper();                        #27
    Alex.turnOff();                           #28

}
```

To verify that this program is correct, we trace the execution of it, carefully simulating the execution of the instructions. Only one instruction can be executed at a time in the robot world. When a program is executing, we call the current instruction the focus of execution. When the helicopter pilot starts to execute a program, the focus is initially on the first instruction within the main task block.

In this sample program the initial focus is the **climbStair** instruction, which is annotated as #1. The **climbStair** message is sent through the satellite to the robot Alex. When Alex receives this message, the focus of execution passes from the pilot to Alex. The pilot, who must wait for the return message that the instruction has been completed, is very careful to remember where he or she was in the program when the **climbStair** message was sent. Alex, upon receiving this message, consults its list of dictionary entries and goes to the definition of **climbStair**. In the sample program the new execution point is annotated as "to here from #1".

Alex focuses on the list of instructions defining the new instruction, **climbStair**, and encounters a **turnLeft** (marked as #2). Alex trains the focus of execution on the **turnLeft** instruction, executes it, and then focuses on #3, **move**. Alex executes this **move** and focuses on #4, **turnRight**. Since this is not a primitive instruction, Alex must retrieve its definition from its dictionary. It then focuses on the instruction list from from definition of **turnRight** and executes the three **turnLeft** instructions, # 5, #6, and #7. Having completed the execution of the **turnRight** instruction, Alex now returns its focus to the place in which the **turnRight** instruction occurred within **climbStair**. Alex shifts focus to #8 and executes the **move**. After Alex performs this **move**, it is finished executing the instruction **climbStair**, so it yields execution to the pilot, since it has completely carried out the task required by the message **climbStair**. The focus of execution returns to the place in the program marked #1, and the pilot sends Alex the **pickBeeper** message that is marked #9. With this message, the focus of execution is again passed from pilot to robot. Alex also interprets and carries out this **pickBeeper** instruction and yields focus back to the pilot at #10. The pilot then sends Alex another **climbStair** instruction. Alex repeats this same sequence of steps a second time for this **climbStair** instruction, marked #10, and the **pickBeeper** that follows, and again for the third **climbStair** and **pickBeeper** instructions. Alex is finally instructed to execute the **turnOff** instruction, and then the program's execution is complete.

Notice that an instruction definition can become Alex's focus from any place in the program that sends Alex that message. The pilot and the robot must always remember where they are in the program when the focus changes. This allows the execution to return to its correct place and continue executing the program. It is important to understand that no complex rules are needed to execute a program containing new instructions. Tracing the execution of this program was a bit tedious because each step is small and simple, but Alex is not equipped to understand anything more complicated. Alex can follow a very simple set of rules that tell it how to execute a program. Yet we can use these simple rules, coupled with every robot's willingness to follow them, to command the robot to perform complicated tasks.

We should now understand how the helicopter pilot and the robots work together to execute a program that includes the instruction definition mechanism. We next turn our attention toward program form, and we make the following observations about the stair-cleaning program.

- We mentioned earlier that declarations are always written before the main task block. In our programming example, we saw that the declaration of the new class and the definition of the new instructions for the class are placed here. We must always write our new instruction definitions in this area. The names defined within a robot class, including the names of the parent class and the parent of the parent, and so on (collectively called <u>ancestors</u>), are called the <u>dictionary</u> of the class. Dictionary entries are always defined in this declaration part of a robot program.

- The declaration of **ur_Robot** does not need to be included in your robot programs, since it is "factory standard." Any other class that you need to define must be completely written in the declaration part, along with the definitions of all of its instructions. We will soon see a shorthand method to make the writing of this dictionary much easier.

- The order of class declarations and instruction definitions is important: Each class must be declared before any of its instructions are defined. Whenever this order is violated, the program has a syntactical error. If two new instructions are introduced in a class declaration, then their definitions may reference each other. This is because definitions of the instructions follow the declaration of the class and therefore the declarations of each of the instructions.

- Each instruction in a block is terminated by a semicolon. Each declaration within a class declaration list is terminated by a semicolon. The class declaration itself is also terminated by a semicolon, but the definition of a new instruction is not. Neither is the main task block.

The class dictionary entries are not permanent, and the world does not remember any definitions from program to program. Each time we write a robot program, we must include a complete set of all dictionary entries required in that program.

## 3.6 MODIFYING INHERITED INSTRUCTIONS

Earlier in this chapter we built the class **Mile_Walker**, which gave robots the ability to walk a mile at a time. Notice that they retained their ability to walk a block at a time as well. Sometimes we want to build a class in which some previously defined instruction is redefined to have a new meaning. For example, suppose we had a problem in which a robot always needed to move by miles but never by blocks. In this case it would be an advantage to create a class with a new definition of the **move** instruction so that when a robot in this class was told to **move**, it would move a mile. This is easily done.

```
class Mile_Mover: ur_Robot
{
        void move();
};

void Mile_Mover::move
{
        ur_Robot::move();
        ur_Robot::move();
        ur_Robot::move();
        ur_Robot::move();
        ur_Robot::move();
        ur_Robot::move();
        ur_Robot::move();
        ur_Robot::move();
}
```

We say that the new definition of **move** in this class <u>overrides</u> the original definition inherited from the class **ur_Robot**. We now have a problem: To move a mile, we need to be able to move eight blocks, but we are defining **move** to mean "move a mile" here. Therefore we can't just say **move** eight times. Instead, we need to indicate that we want to use the original, or <u>overridden</u>, instruction **move** from class **ur_Robot**. We can do this because **ur_Robot** is the parent class. We just need to preface the move instruction with the name of the ancestor class from which we wish to choose the instruction. The scope resolution operator, **::**, is used here to separate the name of a class from the name of its instruction. It gives us a way to specify a particular instruction from a particular class.

Now if we complete the previous program with

```
task
{       Mile_Mover Karel(5, 2, North, 0);
        Karel.move();
        Karel.pickBeeper();
        Karel.move();
        Karel.putBeeper();
        Karel.turnOff();
}
```

Karel will find the beeper at (13, 2) and will leave it at (21, 2).

Notice now that if we had several different robots in the same program and we sent each of them the same messages, they might each respond differently to those messages. In particular, a **Mile_Walker** moves only a block when told to **move**, whereas a **Mile_Mover** moves a mile.

## 3.7   AN UNGRAMMATICAL PROGRAM

Before reading this section, quickly look at the small program in the following example, and see if you can find a syntax error.

This example illustrates the common programming mistake of omitting necessary braces around a block. The program is nicely indented, but the indentation is misleading. The definition of **longMove** appears to define the instruction correctly, but we have omitted the opening brace of the pair that should enclose the three move instructions. Did you spot the mistake? Or were you misled by the other error in this example? Finding the syntax error is not easy because the indentation makes it look correct.

```
class Big_Stepper: ur_Robot
{
        void longMove();
};

void Big_Stepper::longMove()
        move();
        move();
        move();
}

task
{       Big_Stepper Tony;
        Tony.longMove();
```

```
            Tony.turnLeft();
            Tony.turnOff();
}
```

The factory reads the declaration part of a program and the main task block of the program to check for lexical and syntax errors. A reader (human or otherwise) discovers syntax errors by checking "meaningful" components of the program and checking for proper grammar and punctuation. Examples of meaningful components are class declarations, instruction definitions, and the main task block. In effect we verify the meaningful components separately. Let us illustrate how the factory finds the mistake in the preceding program using this examination. Remember that the factory reads only the program's words and is not influenced by the indentation.

The factory examines the new robot class declaration. It has a name, a parent class, and a correct list of features. The punctuation all checks out as well. Then it sees the class name and instruction name in the instruction definition. It then looks for a block to include with the definition, but it doesn't find the opening brace. Instead it finds a name. So the factory says that a syntax error has occurred. In summary, forgetting to use necessary braces around a block can lead to syntax errors.

We are rapidly becoming experts at analyzing programs. Given a robot program, we should now be able to detect grammar and punctuation errors quickly. We should also be able to simulate programs efficiently. Nevertheless, the other side of the programming coin, constructing programs, may still seem a little bit magical. The next few sections take a first step toward demystifying this process.

## 3.8  TOOLS FOR DESIGNING AND WRITING ROBOT PROGRAMS

Designing solutions for problems and writing robot programs involve problem solving. One model[2] describes problem solving as a process that has four activities: defining the problem, planning the solution, implementing the plan, and analyzing the solution.

The initial definition of the problem is presented when we are provided figures of the initial and final situations. Once we examine these situations and understand what task a robot must perform, we begin to plan, implement, and analyze a solution. This section examines techniques for planning, implementing, and analyzing robot programs. By combining these techniques with the new class and instruction mechanism, we can develop solutions that are easy to read and understand.

As we develop and write programs that solve robot problems, these three guidelines must be followed:

- Our programs must be easy to read and understand.
- Our programs must be easy to debug.
- Our programs must be easy to modify to solve variations of the original task.

---

[2]G. Polya, *How to Solve It,* Princeton University Press, 1945, 1973.

### 3.8.1  Stepwise Refinement—A Technique for Planning, Implementing, and Analyzing Robot Programs

This section discusses stepwise refinement, a method to construct robot programs. This method addresses the problem of how we can naturally write concise programs that are correct, simple to read, and easy to understand.

It may appear natural to define all the new classes and instructions needed for a task first, and then write the program using these instructions. But how can we know what robots and which new instructions are needed before we write the program? Stepwise refinement tells us first to write the program using any robots and instruction names we desire, and then define these robots and their instructions. That is, we write the sequence of instructions in the main task block first, and then we write the definitions of the new instruction names used within this block. Finally, we assemble these separate pieces into a complete program.

We will explore this process more concretely by writing a program for the task shown in Figure 3-2. These situations represent a harvesting task that requires a robot to pick up a rectangular field of beepers.

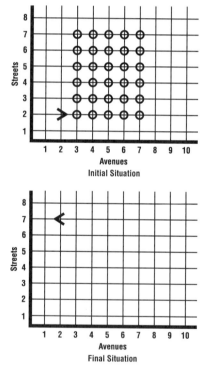

**Figure 3-2**   The Harvest Task

The first step is to develop an overall plan to guide us in writing a robot program that allows Karel to perform the task. Planning is probably best done as a group activity. Sharing ideas in a group allows members to present different plans that can be thoughtfully examined for strengths and weaknesses. Even if we are working alone, we can think in a question-and-answer pattern such as the following.

**Question:** How many robots do we need to perform this task?

**Answer:** We could do it with one robot that walks back and forth over all of the rows to be harvested, or we could do it with a team of robots.

**Question:** How many shall we use?

**Answer:** Let's try it with just one robot, named Mark, for now.

**Question:** How can Mark pick a row?

**Answer:** Mark could move west to east across the southernmost unpicked row of beepers, picking each beeper as it moves.

**Question:** How can Mark pick the entire field?

**Answer:** Mark could turn around and move back to the western side of the field, move north one block, face east, and repeat the actions listed earlier. Mark could do this for each row of beepers in the field. Since Mark is not standing on a beeper we will move it to the first beeper before starting to harvest the first row.

If this idea seems like it might work, the next step is to write out the main task block of the program using English-like new instruction names. We briefly move from planning to implementing our plan. Even though this is done on paper, we should still concentrate on correct syntax and proper indenting to reduce errors when we copy our program into the computer. Suppose we call the class of the new robot by the name **Harvester**.

```
task
{    Harvester Mark(2, 2, East, 0);
     Mark.move();
     Mark.harvestOneRow();
     Mark.returnToStart();
     Mark.moveNorthOneBlock();
     Mark.harvestOneRow();
     Mark.returnToStart();
     Mark.moveNorthOneBlock();
     Mark.harvestOneRow();
     Mark.returnToStart;
     Mark.moveNorthOneBlock();
     Mark.harvestOneRow();
     Mark.returnToStart();
     Mark.moveNorthOneBlock();
     Mark.harvestOneRow();
```

```
        Mark.returnToStart();
        Mark.moveNorthOneBlock();
        Mark.harvestOneRow();
        Mark.returnToStart();
        Mark.turnOff();
    }
```

Notice that what we have really done here is to design a new class of robot that can perform three new instructions. We can think of a robot class as a mechanism for creating service providers: the robots. These robots, examples of objects in object-oriented programming, provide specific services when sent messages requesting the services. Here we seem to require three different services, **harvestOneRow**, **returnToStart**, and **moveNorthOneBlock**, beyond the basic services that all **ur_Robots** can provide.

Before we continue with this plan and begin to work on the new instructions, **harvestOneRow**, **returnToStart**, and **moveNorthOneBlock**, we should analyze our original plan, looking at its strengths and weaknesses. We are asking if we are requesting the **right** services. Our analysis might proceed as follows:

**Question:** What are the strengths of this plan?

**Answer:**   The plan takes advantage of the new instruction mechanism, and it allows Mark to harvest the beepers.

**Question:** What are the weaknesses of the plan?

**Answer:**   Mark makes some "empty" trips.

**Question:** What are these empty trips?

**Answer:**   Mark returns to the starting point on the row that was just harvested.

**Question:** Why are these bad?

**Answer:**   Because robots (and computers) are valuable resources that should generally be used efficiently. Some tasks must be done "on time" if solving them is to confer any benefit.

**Question:** Can Mark pick more beepers on the way back?

**Answer:**   Instead of harvesting only one row and then turning around and returning to the start, Mark can harvest one row, move north one street, and come back to the west, harvesting a second row. Mark can then move one street north to begin the entire process over for the next two rows. If Mark repeats these steps two more times, the entire field of beepers will be harvested.

Again we analyze this new plan for its strengths and weaknesses.

**Question:** What advantage does this offer over the first plan?

**Answer:**   Mark makes only 6 trips across the field instead of 12. There are no empty trips.

**Question:**  What are the weaknesses of this new plan?

**Answer:**   None that we can see as long as there are an even number of rows.

When we are planning solutions, we should be very critical and not just accept the first plan as the best. We now have two different plans, and you can probably think of several more. Let's avoid the empty trips and implement the second plan.

```
task
{       Harvester Mark(2, 2, East, 0);
        Mark.move();
        Mark.harvestTwoRows();
        Mark.positionForNextHarvest();
        Mark.harvestTwoRows();
        Mark.positionForNextHarvest();
        Mark.harvestTwoRows();
        Mark.move();
        Mark.turnOff();
}
```

We must now begin to think about planning the instructions **harvestTwoRows** and **positionForNextHarvest**.


## 3.8.2   The Second Step—Planning harvestTwoRows and positionForNextHarvest

Our plan contains two subtasks: One harvests two rows and the other positions Mark to harvest two more rows. The planning of these two subtasks must be just as thorough as the planning was for the overall task. Let's begin with **harvestTwoRows**.

**Question:**  What does **harvestTwoRows** do?

**Answer:**   **harvestTwoRows** must harvest two rows of beepers. One will be harvested as Mark travels east and the second will be harvested as Mark returns to the west.

**Question:**  What does Mark have to do?

**Answer:**   Mark must pick beepers and move as it travels east. At the end of the row of beepers, Mark must move north one block, face west, and return to the western edge of the field, picking beepers as it travels west.

Continuing to use English-like instruction names, we can now implement this part of the plan.

```
class Harvester: ur_Robot
{
     void harvestTwoRows();
     ...
};

void Harvester::harvestTwoRows()
{
     harvestOneRowMovingEast();
     goNorthToNextRow();
     harvestOneRowMovingWest();
}
```

We analyze this plan as before, looking for strengths and weaknesses.

**Question:** What are the strengths of this plan?

**Answer:** It seems to solve the problem.

**Question:** What are the weaknesses of this plan?

**Answer:** Possibly one—we have two different instructions that harvest a single row of beepers.

**Question:** Do we really need two different harvesting instructions?

**Answer:** We need one for going east and one for going west.

**Question:** Do we really need a separate instruction for each direction?

**Answer:** Harvesting is just a series of **pickBeeper**s and moves. The direction Mark is moving does not matter. If we plan **goToNextRow** carefully, we can use one instruction to harvest a row of beepers when Mark is going east and the same instruction for going west.

Our analysis shows us that we can reuse a dictionary entry (**harvestOneRow**) instead of defining two similar instructions, making our program smaller. Here is the new implementation.

```
void Harvester::harvestTwoRows()
{
     // Before executing this, the robot should be
     //     facing east, on the first beeper of the
     //     current row.
     harvestOneRow();
     goToNextRow();
     harvestOneRow();
}
```

Let's now plan **positionForNextHarvest**.

**Question:** What does the `positionForNextHarvest` instruction do?

**Answer:** This instruction is used when Mark is on the western side of the beeper field. It moves the robot north one block and faces Mark east in position to harvest two more rows of beepers.

**Question:** What does Mark have to do?

**Answer:** Mark must turn right to face north, move one block, and turn right to face east.

We implement this instruction as follows.

```
class Harvester: ur_Robot
{
        void harvestTwoRows();
        void positionForNextHarvest();
        void turnRight();
        ...
};

void Harvester :: positionForNextHarvest()
{
        // Before executing this, the robot should be
        //     facing west, on the last corner
        //     of the current row.
        turnRight();
        move();
        turnRight();
}

void Harvester :: turnRight()
{
        turnLeft();
        turnLeft();
        turnLeft();
}
```

We should analyze this instruction to see whether it works properly. Since it seems to work correctly, we are ready to continue our planning and in the process define more new instructions.

### 3.8.3  The Third Step—Planning `harvestOneRow` and `goToNextRow`

We now focus our efforts on **harvestOneRow** and finally **goToNextRow**.

**Question:** What does **harvestOneRow** do?

**Answer:**   Starting on the first beeper and facing the correct direction, Mark must harvest each of the corners that it encounters, stopping on the location of the last beeper in the row.

**Question:** What does Mark have to do?

**Answer:**   Mark must execute a sequence of **harvestCorner** and **move** instructions to pick all five beepers in the row.

**Question:** How does Mark harvest a single corner?

**Answer:**   Mark must execute a **pickBeeper** instruction.

We can implement **harvestOneRow** and **harvestCorner** as follows.

```
class Harvester: ur_Robot
{
        void harvestTwoRows();
        void positionForNextHarvest();
        void turnRight();
        void harvestOneRow();
        void harvestCorner();
        . . .
};

void Harvester::harvestOneRow()
{
        harvestCorner();
        move();
        harvestCorner();
        move();
        harvestCorner();
        move();
        harvestCorner();
        move();
        harvestCorner();
}

void Harvester::harvestCorner()
{
        pickBeeper();
}
```

We again simulate the instruction, and it seems to work. We now address the instruction **goToNextRow**.

**Question:** What does **goToNextRow** do?

**Answer:**   This instruction moves Mark northward one block to the next row.

**Question:** Didn't we do that already? Why can't we use the instruction `positionForNextHarvest`?[3]

**Answer:** It will not work properly. For `positionForNextHarvest`, Mark must be facing west. Mark is now facing east, so the instruction `positionForNextHarvest` will not work.

**Question:** What does Mark have to do?

**Answer:** Mark must turn left to face north, move one block, and turn left to face west.

The following is the implementation of this new instruction.

```
class Harvester: ur_Robot
{
        void harvestTwoRows();
        void positionForNextHarvest();
        void turnRight();
        void harvestOneRow();
        void goToNextRow();
        . . .
};

void Harvester::goToNextRow()
{
        // Before executing this, the robot should
        //      be facing east, on the last corner of
        //      the current row.
        turnLeft();
        move();
        turnLeft();
}
```

We can use simulation to analyze this instruction and show that it is correct, and our program is done.

## 3.8.4 The Final Step—Verifying that the Complete Program Is Correct

Since we have spread this program out over several pages, it is printed here so that you will find it easier to read and study.

---

[3]At this point you should simulate the instruction `positionForNextHarvest` on paper. Start with Mark facing east and see where the robot is when you finish simulating the instruction.

```
class Harvester: ur_Robot
{
      void harvestTwoRows();
      void positionForNextHarvest();
      void turnRight();
      void harvestOneRow();
      void harvestCorner();
      void goToNextRow();
};

void Harvester::goToNextRow()
{
      turnLeft();
      move();
      turnLeft();
}

void Harvester::harvestOneRow()
{
      harvestCorner();
      move();
      harvestCorner();
      move();
      harvestCorner();
      move();
      harvestCorner();
      move();
      harvestCorner();
}

void Harvester::harvestCorner()
{
      pickBeeper();
}

void Harvester::positionForNextHarvest()
{
      turnRight();
      move();
      turnRight();
}

void Harvester::turnRight()
{
      turnLeft();
      turnLeft();
      turnLeft();
}
```

```
void Harvester::harvestTwoRows
{
     harvestOneRow();
     goToNextRow();
     harvestOneRow();
}

task
{
     Harvester Mark(2, 2, East, 0);
     Mark.move();
     Mark.harvestTwoRows();
     Mark.positionForNextHarvest();
     Mark.harvestTwoRows();
     Mark.positionForNextHarvest();
     Mark.harvestTwoRows();
     Mark.move();
     Mark.turnOff();
}
```

We are not done. We have used simulation to analyze the individual instructions in the program to see whether they work correctly. We have not examined how they work in concert as one large robot program. We must now simulate Mark's execution of the entire program to demonstrate that all the parts work correctly to be sure that the program is correct. We may have relied on some invalid assumptions when writing the instructions that move Mark between rows, or we may discover another error in our planning or implementing; maybe our analysis was wrong. A skeptical attitude toward the correctness of our programs will put us in the correct frame of mind for verifying them.

Stepwise refinement blends the problem-solving activities of planning, implementing, and analyzing into the programming process. It is a powerful programming technique and can shorten the time required to write correct robot programs.

## 3.9   ADVANTAGES OF USING NEW INSTRUCTIONS

It is useful to divide a program into a small set of instructions, even if these instructions are executed only once. New instructions nicely structure programs, and English words and phrases make programs more understandable; they help convey the intent of the program. Read back through the programs we have just written and see if you can find any place where they are confusing or difficult to understand.

We could, of course, use a different plan to solve the preceding (or any) problem. It is useful to think in terms of services required. For instance, in the harvester example, it might be useful to think of **harvestField** as a service. Fulfillment of this service would result in harvesting of an entire field, as the name suggests. We could easily add this feature to the **Harvester** class. Its implementation could be all of the statements of the main task block except the first and last. It would also be possible to create a new class, say **Field_Harvester**, that adds just this new instruction and that is derived from the **Harvester** class.

```
class Field_Harvester: Harvester
{
        void harvestField();
};

void Field_Harvester :: harvestField()
{
        move();
        harvestTwoRows();
        positionForNextHarvest();
        harvestTwoRows();
        positionForNextHarvest();
        harvestTwoRows();
        move();
}
```

Of course, to use this new class we must include its definition, as well as the definition of the **Harvester** class and a main task block, in a single file. One way to do this efficiently is to take advantage of a file inclusion feature of the robot language that we have not used yet. Suppose that we put the previous two definitions in a file named "FHarvest.r" and put the definitions of the **Harvester** class and its instructions in another file, "Harvest.r". Neither file contains a main task block. We could then specify a task within a file, say "Task.r", that contains only the following lines. Separating our robot definitions into separate files makes it easier to reuse them in other programs.

```
#include "Harvest.r"
#include "FHarvest.r"

task
{       Field_Harvester Tony(2, 2, East, 0);
        Tony.harvestField();
        Tony.turnOff();
}
```

The first two lines tell the factory to include the entire contents of Harvest.r and FHarvest.r into this program in place of the include instructions. Notice that the order of these instructions is important since the **Field_Harvester** class defined in FHarvest.r depends on the definitions in Harvest.r, as shown in Figures 3-3(a) and 3–3(b). Using **#include** just tells the factory that it should read another description, such as Harvest.r, at a certain place in a specification.

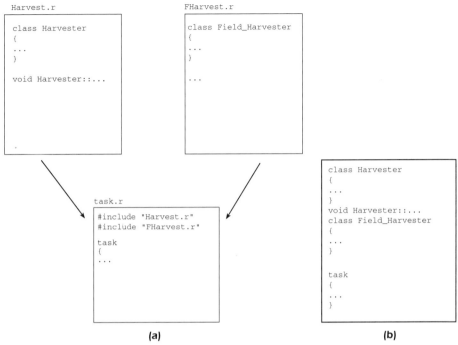

**Figure 3-3**   (a) Using `#include`; This Is What We Write (b) The Effect of Using `#include`; This Is What the Factory Uses

### 3.9.1   Avoiding Errors

Many novices think that all of this planning, analyzing, tracing, and simulating of programs as shown in the previous sections takes too much time. What really takes time is correcting mistakes. These mistakes fall into two broad categories:

- Planning mistakes (execution and intent errors) happen when we write a program without a well-thought-out plan and can waste a lot of programming time. They are usually difficult to fix because large segments of the program may have to be modified or discarded. Careful planning and thorough analysis of the plan can help avoid planning mistakes.

- Programming mistakes (lexical and syntax errors) happen when we actually write the program. They can be spelling, punctuation, or other similar errors. If we write the entire program without testing it, we will undoubtedly have many errors to correct, some of which may be multiple instances of the same mistake. Writing the program in slices will both reduce the overall number of errors introduced at any one time and may prevent multiple occurrences of the same mistake (for example, we discover a misspelling of a new instruction name).

Stepwise refinement is a tool that allows us to plan, analyze, and implement our plans in a way that should lead to a robot program containing a minimum of errors.

### 3.9.2   Future Modifications

Earlier in this chapter we said we must write programs that are easy to read and understand, easy to debug, and easy to modify. The robot's world can be readily changed, and we must be able to modify existing programs to keep the robot out of trouble. It can be much simpler and takes less time to modify an existing program to perform a slightly different task than to write a completely new one. Figures 3-4(a) and 3-4(b) show two situations that differ somewhat from the Harvester task.

How difficult would it be to modify our **Harvester** class and the program containing it to accomplish the new beeper-harvesting tasks? The second problem is easy

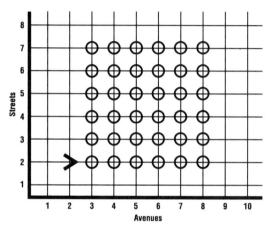

**Figure 3-4(a)**   Longer Rows

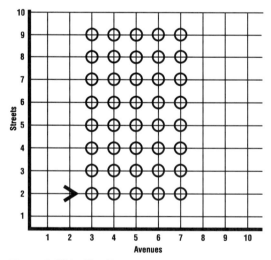

**Figure 3-4(b)**   More Rows

to solve; we just add two new lines to the original main task block to solve the new task. We don't need any changes to the **Harvester** class itself.

What about the first problem? The change here is very different from the change in the second one since we have to pick up an additional beeper in each row. The use of new instructions allows us to quickly find where we need to make the change. There is only one instruction that actually picks up any beepers. We make a simple change to **harvestOneRow** as follows:

```
void Harvester::harvestOneRow()
{
        harvestCorner();
        move();
        harvestCorner();
        move();
        harvestCorner();
        move();
        harvestCorner();
        move();
        harvestCorner();
        move();              // Add these two
        harvestCorner();     // new instructions
}
```

This change to the **Harvester** class is fine provided that we will not need to solve the original problem in the future. It is truly advantageous here to leave the **Harvester** class unchanged and create a new class, **Long_Harvester**, that contains this modified **harvestOneRow** instruction.

```
class Long_Harvester: Harvester
{
        void harvestOneRow();
};

void Long_Harvester::harvestOneRow()
{
        Harvester::harvestOneRow();   // Execute the
                                      // inherited
                                      // instruction
        move();                       // Add these two
        harvestCorner();              // new instructions
}
```

The use of new instructions also simplifies finding and fixing intent errors. This is especially true if the instructions are short and can be easily understood. Suppose our robot makes a wrong turn and tries to pick up a beeper from the wrong place. Where is the error? If we use new instructions to write our program, and each new instruction performs one specific task (such as **positionForNextHarvest**) or controls a set of related tasks (such as **harvestTwoRows**), then we can usually determine the probable location of the error.

### 3.9.3   A Program Without New Instructions

Below is a program that attempts to solve the original beeper-harvesting problem with only primitive instructions. Examine the program and ask the same questions we have just explored.

- Where would we change the program to solve the first modified situation?
- Where would we change the program to solve the second modified situation?
- Suppose Mark makes a wrong turn while planting the beepers. Where would we first look to correct the error?

As an example , find the single error in this program.

```
task
{       ur_Robot Mark(2, 2, East, 0);
        Mark.move();
        Mark.pickBeeper();
        Mark.move();
        Mark.pickBeeper();
        Mark.move();
        Mark.pickBeeper();
        Mark.move();
        Mark.pickBeeper();
        Mark.move();
        Mark.pickBeeper();
        Mark.turnLeft();
        Mark.move();
        Mark.turnLeft();
        Mark.pickBeeper();
        Mark.move();
        Mark.pickBeeper();
        Mark.move();
        Mark.pickBeeper();
        Mark.move();
        Mark.pickBeeper();
        Mark.move();
        Mark.pickBeeper();
        Mark.turnRight();
        Mark.move();
        Mark.turnRight();
        Mark.pickBeeper();
```

```
        Mark.move();
        Mark.pickBeeper();
        Mark.move();
        Mark.pickBeeper();
        Mark.move();
        Mark.pickBeeper();
        Mark.move();
        Mark.pickBeeper();
        Mark.turnRight();
        Mark.move();
        Mark.turnLeft();
        Mark.pickBeeper();
        Mark.move();
        Mark.pickBeeper();
        Mark.move();
        Mark.pickBeeper();
        Mark.move();
        Mark.pickBeeper();
        Mark.move();
        Mark.pickBeeper();
        Mark.turnLeft();
        Mark.move();
        Mark.turnLeft();
        Mark.pickBeeper();
        Mark.move();
        Mark.pickBeeper();
        Mark.move();
        Mark.pickBeeper();
        Mark.move();
        Mark.pickBeeper();
        Mark.move();
        Mark.pickBeeper();
        Mark.move();
        Mark.turnOff();
    }
```

Long lists of instructions such as this may correctly solve a problem, but they are very difficult to read and understand. They are also very difficult to debug and modify.

## 3.10  WRITING UNDERSTANDABLE PROGRAMS

Writing understandable programs is as important as writing correct ones; some say that it is even more important. They argue that most programs initially have a few errors, and understandable programs are easier to debug. Good programmers are distinguished from bad ones by their ability to write clear and concise programs that someone else can read and quickly understand. What makes a program easy to understand? We present two criteria.

- A good program is the simple composition of easily understandable parts. Each part of the programs we just wrote can be understood by itself. Even without a detailed understanding of the parts, the plans that the programs use to accomplish their respective tasks are easy to understand.

- Dividing a program (or a large instruction definition) into small, easy-to-understand pieces is not enough. We must also make sure to name our new instructions properly. These names provide a description, possibly the only description, of what the instruction does. Imagine what the previous programs would look like if for each meaningful instruction name we had used a name like **firstInstruction** or **doItNow**. The robot programming language allows us to choose any instruction names we want, but with this freedom comes the responsibility to select accurate and descriptive names.

It is much easier to verify or debug a program that contains new instructions. The following two facts support this claim.

- New instructions can be independently tested. When writing a program, we should hand-simulate each instruction immediately after it is written until we are convinced that it is correct. Then we can forget how the instruction works and just remember what the instruction does. Remembering should be easy if we name the instruction accurately. This is easiest if the instruction does only one thing.

- New instructions impose a structure on our programs, and we can use this structure to help us find bugs. When debugging a program, we should first find which of the new instructions is malfunctioning. Then we can concentrate on debugging that instruction, ignoring the other parts of our program, which are irrelevant to the bug.

Thus we see that there is an interesting psychological phenomenon related to the robot instruction definition mechanism. Because the human brain can focus on only a limited amount of information at any one time, the ability to ignore details that are no longer relevant is a great aid to program writing and debugging.

To help make our new instruction definitions understandable, we should also keep their lengths within a reasonable range. A good rule of thumb is that definitions should rarely exceed 5 to 10 instructions. This limit leaves enough room to write a meaningful instruction but restrains us from cramming too much detail into any one definition. If an instruction's size exceeds this limit, we should try to divide it naturally into a set of smaller instructions.

This rule applies to the number of instructions written within the main task block, too. Most novice programmers tend to write instruction definitions that are too large. It is better to write many small, well-named instructions instead of a few oversized definitions.

If a new instruction can be executed correctly only in a certain situation, then we should include comments in the definition explaining what those conditions are. For example, an instruction that always picks up a beeper should indicate in a comment where that beeper must appear:

```
void Walker :: stepAndFetchit()
// Requires a beeper on the next corner in front.
{      move();
       pickBeeper();
}
```

Writing understandable programs with new instructions and using the technique of stepwise refinement can reduce the number of errors we make and the amount of time we spend writing robot programs. The real goal, however, is to write **beautiful** programs, programs that other programmers read with enjoyment and we read with satisfaction.

## 3.11 ROBOT TEAMS

In this section we will introduce a very different problem-solving method. Instead of solving a problem with a single robot, suppose we have a team of robots cooperate in the task.

For example, the beeper-harvesting task could be quite easily done by three robots, each sent the message **harvestTwoRows**, if we position them appropriately two blocks apart. The first robot would harvest two rows, then the next robot would harvest the next two rows, and so on. The program would look like the following:

```
#include Harvester

task
{      Harvester Karel(2, 2, East, 0);
       Harvester Kristin (4, 2, East, 0);
       Harvester Matt(6, 2, East, 0);

       Karel.move();
       Karel.harvestTwoRows();
       Karel.turnOff();
       Kristin.move();
       Kristin.harvestTwoRows();
       Kristin.turnOff();
       Matt.move();
       Matt.harvestTwoRows();
       Matt.turnOff();
}
```

The problem could also be solved by six robots, of course.

There is an even more interesting way to do this if we let one robot coordinate the actions of the other two. For this plan to work we need two different kinds of robots. One kind of robot will be called a **Choreographer**, because it directs the others, which can be ordinary, standard-issue **ur_Robot** robots. The trick here is that the Choreographer will set up the others and then will guarantee that they mimic the actions of the Choreographer.

For this to work, the Choreographer needs to know the names of the other two robots, so we will make these names <u>private</u> names of the Choreographer itself. We have not seen this feature of the robot programming language previously. Rather than declare robots in the main task block, we can define robot names within a new class. Robots declared like this will be available as helpers to robots of the class being declared but may not be used by other robots or in the main task block. This is because the names of the helper robots will be private to the robot of the new class.

The Choreographer will also need to override all of the robot instructions so that, for example, if we tell the Choreographer to move, it can direct the others to move as well.

```
class Choreographer: ur_Robot
{
        ur_Robot Lisa(4, 2, East, 0);
        // the first helper robot
        ur_Robot Tony(6, 2, East, 0);
        // the second helper robot
        void harvest();
        void harvestARow();
        void harvestCorner();
        void move();
        void pickBeeper();
        void turnLeft();
        void turnOff();
};
```

Here is the main task block for our program.

```
task
{       Choreographer Karel(2, 2, East, 0);
        Karel.harvest();
        Karel.turnOff();
}
```

**Harvest** and **harvestARow** are similar to what we have seen before.

```
void Choreographer::harvest()
{
        harvestARow();
        turnLeft();
```

```
        move();
        turnLeft();
        harvestARow();
}

void Choreographer::harvestARow()
{
        move();
        harvestCorner();
        move();
        harvestCorner();
        move();
        harvestCorner();
        move();
        harvestCorner();
        move();
        harvestCorner();
        move();
}

void Choreographer::harvestCorner()
{
        pickBeeper();
}
```

The key to making a Choreographer and its team work together is in redefining the inherited instructions. The other instructions are very similar to each other. We show only **move** here.

```
void Choreographer::move()
{
        ur_Robot::move();
        Lisa.move();
        Tony.move();
}
```

Each of the other instructions first executes the inherited instruction of the same name and then sends the message to the two helper robots.

Notice that when asked to move, the Choreographer robot (here Karel) first executes the inherited **move** instruction to **move** itself and then sends **move** instructions to the two helpers, which are only **ur_Robot**s, so they don't affect any other robots. This means that whenever Karel moves, each of its helpers also moves "automatically." The same will be true for **pickBeeper** and the **turnLeft** instruction. When a robot sends a message to another robot, the message passes from the sender of the message through the satellite to the other robot. The sender must then wait for the completion of the instruction by the robot to which it sent the message before it can resume its own execution.

Be sure to trace the execution of this program. Notice that the order of execution of this solution is very different from the first solution given in this section.

## 3.12    OBJECT-ORIENTED DESIGN

In Section 3.8 we learned a useful technique for designing a single class by asking what tasks are needed from that class and designing complex tasks as a decomposition into simpler tasks. Now we are going to look at design from a broader perspective. Here we recognize that we may need several classes of robots to carry out some task, and these robots may need to cooperate in some way. Here we will discuss only the design issues, leaving implementation until we have seen the powerful instructions of the next two chapters.

Suppose that we want to build a robot house as shown in Figure 3-5. Houses will be built of beepers, of course. In the real world, house building is a moderately complex task that is usually done by a team of builders, each with his or her own specialty. Perhaps it should be the same in the robot world.

If you look back at some of our earlier examples, you will find that there are really two kinds of instructions. The first kind of instruction, such as **Harvester::harvestTwoRows**, is meant to be used in the main task block. The other kind, such as **Harvester::goToNextRow**, is meant primarily to be used internally, as part of problem decomposition. For example, the instruction **Harvester::goToNextRow** is unlikely to be used except from within other instructions. The first kind of instruction is meant to be public and defines in some way what the robot is intended to do. If we think of a robot as a <u>server</u>, then its <u>client</u> (the main task block,

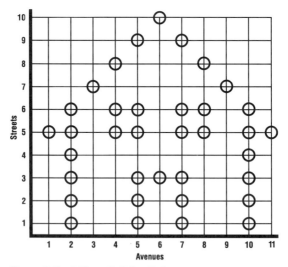

**Figure 3-5**    A House-Building Task

or perhaps another robot) will send it a message with one of its "public" instructions. The client is one who requests a service from a server. A Harvester robot provides a harvesting service. Its client requests that service. The place to begin design is with the public services and the servers that provide them. The server robot itself will then, perhaps, execute other instructions to provide the service. We can use successive refinement to help design the other instructions that help the server carry out its service.

The easiest way to get a house built is to call on the services of a <u>contractor</u>, who will assemble some appropriate team to build our house. We tell the contractor robot **buildHouse** and somehow the job gets done. The client doesn't especially care how the contractor carries out the task as long as the results (including the price) are acceptable. (Here the costs are low, since robots don't need to send their children to college.) Notice that we have just given the preliminary design for a class, the **Contractor** class, with one public instruction: **buildHouse**. We may discover the need for more instructions and for more classes as well. We also know that we will probably need only a single robot of the **Contractor** class. Let's name it Kristin.

Now we examine the task from Kristin's standpoint. What does it need to do to build a house? One possibility is to place all of the beepers itself. But another way is to use specialist robots to handle well-defined parts of the house, for example, walls, the roof, and the doors and windows. We want the walls to be made of bricks (beeper-bricks, that is), so we should call on the services of one or more mason robots. The doors and windows could be built by a pair of carpenter robots, and the roof built by a roofer robot.

The contractor, Kristin, needs to be able to gather this team, so we need another instruction for this. It could be called by the client, or could be called internally by the contractor itself when it is ready to begin construction. Kristin also needs to be able to get the team to the construction site. We will want a new instruction, **Contractor::gatherTeam**.

Focusing, then, on the smaller jobs, the mason robot should be able to respond to a **buildWall** message. The contractor can show the mason where the walls are to be built. Similarly, the roofer should be able to respond to **makeRoof**, and the carpenter robots should know the messages **makeDoor** and **makeWindow**. We might go a step further with the roofer and decide that it would be helpful to make the two gables of the roof separately. So we would also want a **Roofer::makeLeftGable** and **Roofer::makeRightGable**.

```
class Mason: ur_Robot
{
        void buildWall();
};

void Mason :: buildWall()
{
        ...
}

class Carpenter: ur_Robot
```

```
{
        void makeWindow();
        void makeDoor();
};
void Carpenter::makeWindow()
{
        ...
}
void Carpenter::makeDoor()
{
        ...
}
class Roofer: ur_Robot
{
        void makeRoof();
        void makeLeftGable();
        void makeRightGable();
};
void Roofer::makeRoof()
{
        ...
}
void Roofer::makeLeftGable()
{
        ...
}
void Roofer::makeRightGable()
{
        ...
}
```

This gives us an outline for the helper classes. Let's look again at the **Contractor** class. Since the team of builders is assembled by the contractor, it must know their names. Therefore it would be useful if the names of the helpers were declared as private names in the **Contractor** class itself, rather than global names. This will also effectively prevent the client of the contractor from telling the workers directly what to do.

```
class Contractor: ur_Robot
{
        Mason Ken_the_Mason(1,1,E,??);
        Roofer Sue_the_Roofer(...);
```

```
        Carpenter Linda_the_Carpenter(...);
        Carpenter Steve_the_Carpenter(...);

        void gatherTeam();
        void buildHouse();
};

void Contractor::gatherTeam()        // Call prior to
                                     // first move.
{
        // Instructions here for initial positioning
        // of the team.
}

void Contractor::buildHouse()
{
        // Instructions here to the four workers.

}

task
{       Contractor Kristin(1, 1, East, 0);
        ...
        Kristin.buildHouse();
        ...
        Kristin.turnOff();
}
```

Note that the contractor is a server. Its client is the main task block. But note also that Kristin is a client of the four helpers since they provide services (wall services, for example) to Kristin. In fact it is relatively common in the real world for clients and servers to be mutually bound. For example, doctors provide medical services to grocers who provide food marketing services to doctors.

## 3.13  PROBLEM SET

The problems in this section require defining new instructions for a robot named Karel, or writing complete programs that include such new instructions. Concentrate on writing well-structured programs, built from naturally descriptive new instructions. Practice using stepwise refinement and freely define any new instructions that you need. If you find yourself continually writing the same sequence of instructions, it is a sure sign that you need to define that sequence as a new instruction. Carefully check for syntax errors in your program, and simulate Karel's execution of each program to verify that it is correct.

Paradoxically, the programs in this problem set will be among the largest you will write. The instructions covered in the next chapters are so powerful that we will find that complex tasks can be solved with programs comprising a small number of these potent instructions.

1. Write appropriate definitions for the following instructions: (1) **moveMile**, remembering that miles are eight blocks long; (2) **move_backward**, which moves Karel one block backward, but leaves it facing the same direction; and (3) **move_kilo_mile**, which moves Karel 1000 miles forward. This last problem is difficult, but a fairly short solution does exist. You may use the **moveMile** instruction in this problem without redefining it. Can any of these instructions cause an error shutoff when it is executed?

2. Karel sometimes works as a pin-setter in a bowling alley. Write a program that instructs Karel to transform the initial situation in Figure 3-6 into the final situation. Karel starts this task with ten beepers in its beeper-bag.

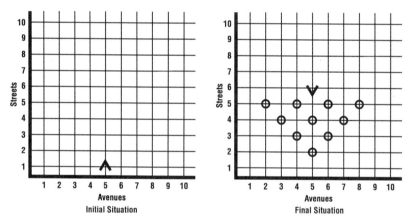

**Figure 3-6** A Pin-Setting Task

3. Rewrite the harvesting program using a different stepwise refinement.

4. Figure 3-7 illustrates a field of beepers that Karel planted one night after a baseball game. Write a program that harvests all these beepers. *Hint:* This task is not too different from the harvesting example. If you see the correspondence between these two harvesting tasks, you should be able to develop a program for this task that is similar to the original harvesting program.

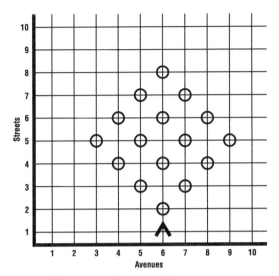

**Figure 3-7** Another Harvesting Task

5. Karel wants to send greetings to the other inhabitants of the universe, so the robot needs to plant a field of beepers that broadcasts the message to alien astronomers. Program Karel to plant the message of beepers shown in Figure 3-8. You may choose Karel's starting position.

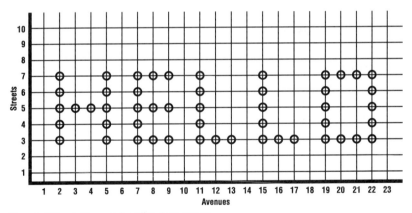

**Figure 3-8** A Message for Alien Astronomers

6. Redo Problem 5, but this time use five robots, one for each letter to be written. You may choose each robot's starting position.

7. Redo Problem 5, but this time use five robots, one for each street.

8. Redo Problem 5, but this time use 17 robots, one for each avenue.

9. Karel has received a contract from NASA (the National Aeronautics and Space Administration of the United States) to display the correct time for astronauts to read as they orbit above Karel's world. The time must be displayed digitally and must fit in the situation shown in Figure 3-9. You may choose the size and shape of the digits. The program must allow you to change the time quickly so Karel can rapidly update the display. For practice, display the time 10:52.

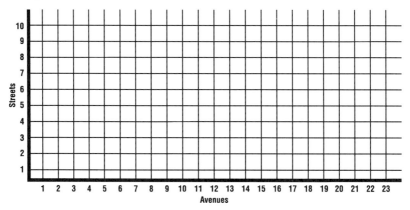

**Figure 3-9**   A Digital Clock

10. Redo Problem 9, using five robots, one for each digit and one for the colon.

11. Karel has taken a part-time job as a gardener. Karel's specialty is planting beepers. Karel's current task is to plant one and only one beeper on each corner around the "+"-shaped wall arrangement as shown in the situation in Figure 3-10.

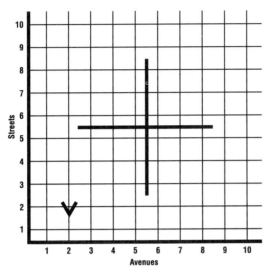

**Figure 3-10** A Gardening Task

**12.** Redo Problem 11 with four robots. You may choose the starting position of each robot.

**13.** Redo Problem 11 with eight robots. You may choose the starting position of each robot.

**14.** Redo Problem 11 with a Choreographer and three helpers. You may choose the starting position of each robot.

**15.** Karel became bored with gardening, so the robot decided to try a different part-time job. The robot now installs carpets (made from beepers) in buildings in its world. Write a program that instructs Karel to install a carpet in the building shown in Figure 3-11. There must be no "lumps" in the carpet, so be sure that Karel places one and only one beeper on each intersection in the room.

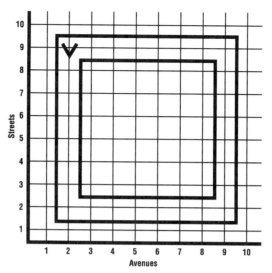

**Figure 3-11**   A Carpet Task

16. Program Karel to arrange beepers as shown in the final situation given in Figure 3-12. Karel has exactly 12 beepers in its beeper bag. You may start Karel on any convenient corner.

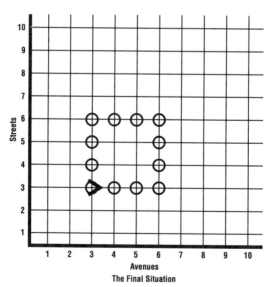

**The Final Situation**

**Figure 3-12**   A Box of Beepers

17. Give a specification for a class in which (1) the new robots have all of the capabilities of robots in class **ur_Robot**, and (2) they can also execute the instruction **pickAPair**, which will cause such a robot to pick up two beepers (if available) from the current corner. Call this new class **Pick_a_Pair_Robot**. Give the specification for this new class in the robot programming language.

18. Solve the harvester problem again using a team of six robots. Each robot can harvest a single row.

# 4 CONDITIONALLY EXECUTING INSTRUCTIONS

In the preceding chapters, a robot's exact initial situation was known at the start of a task. When we wrote our programs, this information allowed Karel to find beepers and avoid running into walls. However, these programs worked only in their specific initial situations. If a robot tried to execute one of these programs in a slightly different initial situation, the robot would almost certainly perform an error shutoff.

What a robot needs is the ability to survey its local environment and then decide from that information what to do next. The IF instructions are discussed in this chapter. There are two versions of the IF statement: the IF and the IF/ELSE. They provide robots with their decision ability. Both allow a robot to test its environment and, depending on the result of the test, decide which instruction to execute next. The IF instructions enable us to write much more general programs for our robots that accomplish the same task in a variety of similar, but different, initial situations.

Robot programs contain several different kinds of instructions. The first, and most important, is the message to a robot. These messages are sent to robots either by the pilot (when they appear in the main task block) or by another robot (when they occur in an instruction of some class). The action associated with this kind of instruction is defined by the corresponding instruction in the class of the robot to which the message is directed.

Another kind of instruction is the delivery specification, which is sent to the factory to construct a new robot and have the helicopter pilot deliver it.

The IF instruction is yet another different kind of instruction. The rest of this chapter and the next are going to add to this list of kinds of instructions.

## 4.1 THE IF INSTRUCTION

The IF instruction is the simpler of the two IF variants. It has the following general form:

```
if ( < test > )
{
        < instruction-list >
}
```

The IF instruction introduces the new reserved word **if** (spelled in lowercase). The reserved word **if** signals a program reader that an IF instruction is present, and the braces enclose a list of instructions. The < instruction-list > is known as the THEN clause of the instruction. We indent the IF instruction as shown to highlight the fact that < instruction-list > is a component of the IF instruction. Note that we do not follow the right brace of an IF instruction with a semicolon.

A robot executes the IF instruction by first checking whether < test > contained in the parentheses is true or false in the robot's current situation. If < test > is true, the robot executes < instruction-list >; if < test > is false, the robot skips < instruction-list >. In either case, the robot is then finished executing the entire IF instruction. For an example, let's look at the program fragment[1] below, which consists of an IF instruction followed by a **turnLeft** instruction. Assume that this fragment is contained in an instruction of some class. Some robot of that class will be executing the code.

```
if ( nextToABeeper())
{
        pickBeeper();
}
turnLeft();
```

When this IF instruction is executed by the robot, it first checks whether it is next to (on the same corner as) a beeper. If it finds that **nextToABeeper** is true, the robot executes the THEN clause, which instructs it to execute **pickBeeper**. The robot is now finished executing the IF instruction, and continues by executing the rest of the instructions, starting at the **turnLeft** instruction.

Now suppose that there are no beepers on the corner when the robot executes this program fragment. In this case **nextToABeeper** is false, so the robot does not execute the THEN clause. Instead, it skips directly to the **turnLeft** instruction and continues executing the program from there. The result of this second case is that the robot executes the IF instruction by doing nothing more than asking itself to check whether or not it is next to a beeper. An error shutoff cannot occur in either case, because the robot executes the **pickBeeper** instruction only if it confirms the presence of at least one beeper on the corner.

It is also possible to use IF statements in the main task block, but here we must be careful to ask a particular robot about its state. We ask about a robot's state by sending messages, just as we ask robots to perform instructions using messages. If we want to

---

[1]To conserve space, we often demonstrate a programming idea without writing a complete robot program or new instruction. Instead, we just write the necessary instructions, which are called a <u>program fragment</u>.

know about the state of a particular robot we must send a message to that robot. When we don't name any robot at all, we are asking about the state of the robot actually executing the current instruction. Since the main task block is not an instruction of any robot class, we must use a robot's name there.

```
if ( Karel.nextToABeeper())
{
        Karel.pickBeeper();
}
Karel.turnLeft();
```

## 4.2 THE CONDITIONS THAT ROBOTS CAN TEST

In Chapter 1 we briefly discussed the sensory capabilities of robots. We learned that a robot can see walls, hear beepers, determine which direction it is facing, and feel whether there are any beepers in its beeper-bag or other robots on its current corner. The conditions that a robot can test are divided according to these same four categories.

Following is a new class, with several conditions that robots of this class can test. This class can serve as the parent class of many of your own classes for the remainder of your visit to Karel's world. The class is so important, in fact, that the Karel-Werke makes its definition available to all robot purchasers. Therefore you may use this class in the same way that you use **ur_Robot**. You don't need to type it or even **#include** it. Since these are the most common type of robot, the name of the class is simply **Robot**. These robots will be able to make good use of IF and other similar statements.

```
class Robot: ur_Robot
{
        Boolean frontIsClear();
        Boolean nextToABeeper();
        Boolean nextToARobot();
        Boolean facingNorth();
        Boolean facingSouth();
        Boolean facingEast();
        Boolean facingWest();
        Boolean anyBeepersInBeeperBag();
};
```

The items in the instruction list name the tests that a robot of the Robot class may perform using its sensors. They return true or false values to the robot mechanism and so we mark them as **Boolean**.[2] These instructions are called <u>predicates</u>. They

---

[2]Boolean instructions are named after George Boole, one of the early developers of logic.

provide the means by which robots can be queried (or can query their own internal state) to decide whether certain conditions are true or false. On the other hand, actions such as **move** and **turnOff** are flagged as **void** because the robot gets no feedback information from them. The word **void** indicates the absence of a returned value. In computer programming languages, parts of a program that have a value are called expressions. Expressions are usually associated with a type, giving the valid values of the expression. A predicate represents a Boolean expression, meaning that its value is either **true** or **false**.

Robot programmers can create new predicates in their own classes, just as they can create new instructions.

Recall that robots have a microphone that they can use to listen and determine if there are any beepers present on their current corner. This action is activated by the **nextToABeeper** message. If a robot, say Carol, is sent the message **Carol.nextToABeeper()**, it will activate the microphone and will respond to the message with **true** or **false**. The state of the robot doesn't change, but the sender of the message will obtain information about the state of the robot. This information can be put to use only by statements such as the IF instruction and others in this and the next chapter. The **nextToABeeper** test is true when a robot is on the same corner as one or more beepers. A robot cannot hear beepers any farther away, and it cannot hear beepers that are in the soundproof beeper-bag.

The **nextToARobot** predicate is similar and returns whether or not there is another robot on the same corner. This predicate activates the robot's arm, which is used to feel about for other robots.

Remember that each robot has a TV camera for eyes, focused to detect a wall exactly one-half of a block away to the front. This camera is facing directly ahead. The **frontIsClear** predicate tests this condition. If a robot needs to test if its right is clear, it will need to proceed by first turning to the right to check for the presence of a wall. It can then return to its original orientation by turning back to its left.

A robot consults its internal compass to decide what direction it is facing. Finally, a robot can test whether or not there are any beepers in the beeper-bag by probing it with the mechanical arm. This condition is returned by the **anyBeepersInBeeperBag** predicate.

We will often want both positive and negative forms of many predicates. For example, we would probably want a predicate **frontIsBlocked** as the negative form of **frontIsClear**. Only the positive forms are provided by the Robot class, however. To aid in the writing of such negative forms, we will rely on the logical negation operator. In English this is usually written not. In the robot programming language we use the negation operator, "!", for this. For example, we have **nextToABeeper**; if we also want "not **nextToABeeper**", what we write is **! nextToABeeper()**. Any message evaluating a predicate can be "negated" by preceding it with the negation operator "!" (sometimes called "bang"). Thus, if robot Karel has beepers in its beeper-bag, then it could respond to the instruction

```
if (! Karel.nextToABeeper())
{
//Read: ''If it is not true that Karel is next to
```

```
//a beeper . . .''
     Karel.putBeeper();
}
```

Alternatively, we could create our own subclass of the Robot class and provide a new predicate **not_nextToABeeper**, as shown in the next section. In this case we would use

```
if ( Karel.not_nextToABeeper())
{
     Karel.putBeeper();
}
```

## 4.2.1  Writing New Predicates

The eight predicates just defined are built into the language, but the user can also write new predicates. Predicates return Boolean values **true** and **false**. Therefore, in the block of the definition of a new predicate, we need to indicate what value is to be returned. For this we need a new kind of instruction: the RETURN instruction. The form of the RETURN instruction is the reserved word **return**, followed by an expression. In a Boolean instruction the value of the expression must be true or false. RETURN instructions are legal only in predicates. They cannot be used in ordinary (void) instructions or in the main task block.

We might want predicates that are negative forms of the Robot class predicates. They can be defined using the not operator. For example, in a class **Checker_Robot**, we might want the following as well as some others:

```
Boolean Checker_Robot :: frontIsBlocked()
{
     return ! frontIsClear();
}
```

Then when a **Checker_Robot** is asked if its **frontIsBlocked**, it executes the RETURN instruction. To do this it must first evaluate the **frontIsClear** predicate, receiving an answer of either true or false. It then returns the negative of this because of the negation operator. Therefore if **frontIsClear** returns **false**, and if this is negated, then **frontIsBlocked** returns **true**. We can similarly write **not_nextToABeeper**.

```
Boolean Checker_Robot :: not_nextToABeeper()
{
     return ! nextToABeeper();
}
```

We might want to "extend" a robot's vision by providing a test for **rightIsClear**. This instruction is much more complicated since robots have no sensor to their right.

One solution is to face toward the right so that the forward sensor may be used. However, we shouldn't leave the robot facing that new direction, since the name of the instruction (`rightIsClear`) does not seem to imply any change in direction. Therefore we should be sure to return to the original direction before returning the value. Therefore `rightIsClear` must execute turn instructions in addition to returning a value.

```
Boolean Checker_Robot :: rightIsClear()
{
        turnRight();
        if ( frontIsClear() )
        {
                turnLeft();
                return true;
        }
        turnLeft();
        return false;
}
```

The return instruction immediately terminates the predicate that contains it. Therefore, if `frontIsClear` is true then the robot will turn left and return `true`. This instruction will have then terminated (returned). It won't reach or execute the second `turnLeft` or the `return false` instruction. On the other hand, if the `frontIsClear` test returns false, then the robot skips the THEN clause, and so it executes the second `turnLeft` and the `return false` instruction. Notice that we were careful here to leave the robot facing the same direction that it was facing before this predicate was executed. Therefore the programmer using `rightIsClear` can ignore the fact that the robot executes turns in order to evaluate this predicate, since any turn is undone. We can say that the turn is "transparent" to the user.

Notice that in the `rightIsClear` instruction, if we reverse the order of the last two instructions in the body, then the return instruction will be executed before the `turnLeft` (only when `frontIsClear()` is false, of course). But because the return will terminate the predicate, we won't ever execute the `turnLeft`. This would be an error, since it wouldn't leave the robot facing the original direction as was intended.

## 4.3 SIMPLE EXAMPLES OF THE IF INSTRUCTION

This section examines three new instructions that use the IF instruction. During our discussion we will also consider how IF instructions are checked for correctness.

### 4.3.1 The harvestOneRow Instruction

Let's give Karel a new task similar to the harvesting task discussed in Section 3.8.1. Karel's new task still requires the robot to harvest the same size field, but this time there is no guarantee that a beeper is on each corner of the field. Because Karel's original program for this task would cause an error shutoff when it tried to execute a **pickBeeper** on any barren corner, we must modify it to avoid executing illegal **pickBeeper** instructions. Karel must harvest a beeper only if it determines that one is present.

Knowing about the new IF instruction, we can now write a program for this slightly more general task. One sample initial situation is illustrated in Figure 4–1.

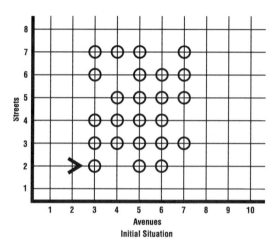

**Figure 4–1** A Modified Harvest Task—Not All Corners Have Beepers

Please notice that this is only one of many possible initial situations. Our program must be able to harvest this size field (six by five) regardless of which corners have beepers and which corners do not.

Luckily for us, most of our previously written harvesting program can be reused—another advantage of object-oriented programming with classes. All we need to do is to create a new version of the **harvestCorner** instruction in a new subclass of **Harvester**. The new version of **harvestCorner** picks up a beeper only if it knows there is one on the current corner. To do this we create a new class, **Sparse_Harvester**, whose parent class is **Harvester**. We will also, however, need to modify **Harvester** so that its parent class is **Robot** rather than **ur_Robot**. With this change we can take advantage of the predicates defined in class **Robot**.

```
#include "Harvester.r"
class Sparse_Harvester: Harvester
{
        void harvestCorner();
};
```

Of course, we must also write the **harvestCorner** instruction, but this is easily done by using the IF instruction.

```
void Sparse_Harvester:: harvestCorner()
{
    if ( nextToABeeper() )
    {
        pickBeeper();
    }
}
```

## 4.3.2  The `faceNorthIfFacingSouth` Instruction

This section will demonstrate how we decide when to use the IF instruction and how we decide what condition we want a robot to check in < test >. As part of this discussion and future discussions, let's assume we are planning and implementing the solution to a large problem in which a robot named Karel is on a treasure hunt for the Lost Beeper Mine, which is a very large pile of beepers.

Let's further assume that we have developed an overall plan and are working on one small task within this plan. This task requires that Karel face to the north only if it is currently facing south. In Chapter 3 we introduced a question-and-answer format to show how we might plan and analyze possible ways to solve a problem. The same format also works well in the implementing phase of problem solving.

**Question:**  What does Karel have to do?

**Answer:**    Karel must turn to face north only if it is currently facing south.

**Question:**  How many alternatives does the robot have to choose from?

**Answer:**    Two.

**Question:**  What are these alternatives?

**Answer:**    Alternative 1 is to turn to the north if it is facing south. Alternative 2 is to do nothing if it is facing any other direction.

**Question:**  What instruction can we use to allow Karel to decide which alternative to choose?

**Answer:**    The IF instruction allows Karel to decide which alternative to choose.

**Question:**  What test can Karel use in the IF instruction?

**Answer:**    Karel is supposed to turn to the north only if it is facing to the south, so the `facingSouth` test can be used.

**Question:**  What does Karel do if it is facing south?

**Answer:**    Karel will `turnLeft` twice.

**Question:**  What does Karel do if it is not facing south?

**Answer:**    Karel does nothing.

The thought process for implementing each instruction definition in our program must be as careful and detailed as it was when we were developing our original plan for the solution. Each step must be carefully analyzed for its strengths and weaknesses. If we ask a question and we cannot answer it satisfactorily, then either we have asked the wrong question or our plan for the instruction's definition is flawed. The longer we spend thinking about the implementation, the less time we will spend correcting errors. Having taken the time to analyze our answers, our instruction implementation looks like this. We assume here that we are building a new class of robots, **Prospector**, that can search for the Lost Beeper Mine.

```
void Prospector::faceNorthIfFacingSouth()
{
     if (facingSouth())
     {
          turnLeft();
          turnLeft();
     }
}
```

### 4.3.3  The `faceNorth` Instruction

Here is a new problem to solve. Let's assume we are planning the definition of another part of the Lost Beeper Mine problem. We must implement an instruction definition that faces a robot north regardless of the direction it is currently facing. Using the question-and-answer format, we approach this solution by first thinking about Karel's situation. Can we use the information about the direction Karel is currently facing to solve the problem?

**Question:**  What does Karel have to do?

**Answer:**  It must determine which direction it is facing to decide how many **turnLefts** to execute so it will be facing north.

**Question:**  How many different alternatives does the robot have?

**Answer:**  Karel has one alternative for each direction it could be facing. Therefore it has four alternatives.

**Question:**  What are these alternatives?

**Answer:**  Alternative 1, facing north—do nothing.
Alternative 2, facing east—turn left once.
Alternative 3, facing south—turn left twice.
Alternative 4, facing west—turn left three times.

**Question:**  What test(s) can Karel use to decide which direction it is facing?

**Answer:**    Karel can check to see if it is `facingEast`, `facingSouth`, `facingWest`—since Karel does not have to do anything when it is facing north, we do not have to use that test.

We can use these questions and their answers to aid us in implementing the new instruction `faceNorth`.

```
void Prospector :: faceNorth()
{
        if (facingEast())
        {
                turnLeft();
        }
        if (facingSouth())
        {
                turnLeft();
                turnLeft();
        }
        if (facingWest())
        {
                turnLeft();
                turnLeft();
                turnLeft();
        }
}
```

Compare this instruction to the set of questions preceding it. Did we ask all of the necessary questions? Did we answer them correctly? Trace this instruction for execution and simulate it four times, one for each direction Karel could initially be facing. Does it work in all cases?

There is another way to solve this problem. Examine this set of questions.

**Question:**    What does Karel have to do?

**Answer:**    Karel must `turnLeft` until it is facing north.

**Question:**    How many alternatives does the robot have?

**Answer:**    Two.

**Question:**    What are they?

**Answer:**    Alternative 1 is to `turnLeft` if it is not facing north.
Alternative 2 is to do nothing if it is already facing north.

**Question:**    How can we use this information?

**Answer:**    Karel can never be more than three `turnLeft`s away from facing north, so we can use a sequence of three IF instructions; each one will check to see if Karel is not **facingNorth**. If the test is true, Karel will **turnLeft** and be one left turn closer to facing north.

**Question:**  What happens when Karel starts out facing north?

**Answer:**  All three tests will be false and Karel does nothing.

**Question:**  What happens when Karel is facing east?

**Answer:**  The first test is true, and Karel executes a **turnLeft**. The remaining two tests are false and Karel does nothing.

**Question:**  What happens when Karel is facing south?

**Answer:**  The first two tests are true, so Karel executes two **turnLefts**. The third test is false and its THEN clause is skipped.

**Question:**  What happens when Karel is facing west?

**Answer:**  All three tests will be true, so Karel will execute three **turnLefts**.

Here is our resulting new instruction.

```
void Prospector :: faceNorth()
{
        if ( ! facingNorth() )
        {
                turnLeft();
        }
        if ( ! facingNorth() )
        {
                turnLeft();
        }
        if ( ! facingNorth() )
        {
                turnLeft();
        }
}
```

Trace this instruction for execution and simulate it four times, one for each direction Karel could initially be facing. Does it work in all cases?

The question must be asked as to which of these two faceNorth instructions is better. For now, either is perfectly acceptable.

## 4.3.4  Determining the Correctness of the IF Instruction

Checking an IF instruction is similar to checking a dictionary entry; both are "meaningful" components of a program. Both IF instructions and dictionary entries use reserved words and braces to separate their different parts. You check the IF instruction by first checking the $<$ test $>$, making sure it is correct and contained in parentheses. You then check the instructions inside the braces. Finally, you check the entire IF instruction including its braces.

Study, for example, the version of **captureTheBeeper** that follows.

```
void Game_Player :: captureTheBeeper()
{
        move();
        if (nextToABeeper())
        {
                pickBeeper();
                turnAround();
        }
        move();
}
```

This definition contains three instructions: the first **move**, the IF, and the second **move**. The **move** instructions are terminated by semicolons, and the two instructions inside the block of the IF are likewise terminated by semicolons. The predicate is correct and is contained in parentheses, and the braces for the IF correctly enclose the two instructions. It seems fine. Notice, however, that it leaves us in one of two different places, facing in one of two different directions, depending on whether it finds a beeper or not. It might be important in some problems to avoid this difference because other instructions will be executed after this one. If we are not careful, the robot could wander away from the desired path. We try to be careful to pick a name for an instruction that describes all that the robot will do when executing it. We also generally try to leave the robot in the same state regardless of how it executes the instruction. The next instruction will help in this.

## 4.4  THE IF/ELSE INSTRUCTION

In this section we discuss the second type of IF instruction built into the robot vocabulary. The IF/ELSE instruction is useful when, depending on the result of some test, a robot must execute one of two alternative instructions. The general form of the IF/ELSE is as follows:

```
if ( <test> )
{
            < instruction-list-1 >
}
else
{
            < instruction-list-2 >
}
```

The form of the IF/ELSE is similar to the IF instruction, except that it includes an ELSE clause. Note the absence of a semicolon before the word *else* and at the end. A robot executes an IF/ELSE in much the same manner as an IF. It first determines whether < test > is true or false in the current situation. If < test > is true, the robot executes < instruction-list-1 >; if < test > is false, it executes < instruction-list-2 >. Thus, depending on its current situation, the robot executes either < instruction-list-1 > or < instruction-list-2 >, but not both. By the way, the first instruction list in an IF/ELSE instruction is called the THEN clause, and the second instruction list is called the ELSE clause.

Let's look at a task that uses the IF/ELSE instruction. Suppose that we want to program a robot to run a 1-mile-long hurdle race, where vertical wall sections represent hurdles. The hurdles are only one block high and are randomly placed between any two corners in the race course. One of the many possible race courses for this task is illustrated in Figure 4–2. Here we think of the world as being vertical, with down being south. We require the robot to jump if, and only if, faced with a hurdle.

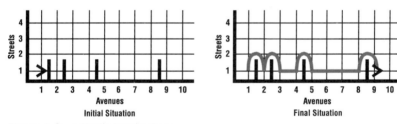

**Figure 4–2** A Hurdle-Jumping Race

The robot could easily program this race by jumping between every pair of corners, but although this strategy is simple to program, it doesn't meet the requirements. (Perhaps it would slow the robot down too much.) Instead, we must program the robot to move straight ahead when it can, and jump over hurdles only when it must. The program implementing this strategy consists of a main task block that contains eight **raceStride** instructions followed by a **turnOff**. The definition of **raceStride** can be written using stepwise refinement as follows.

```
void Racer :: raceStride()
{
        if ( frontIsClear() )
        {
                move();
        }
        else
        {
                jumpHurdle();
        }
}
```

We continue our refinement by writing **jumpHurdle**.

```
void Racer :: jumpHurdle()
{
        jumpUp();
        move();
        glideDown();
}
```

Finally, we write **jumpUp** and **glideDown**, the instructions needed to complete the definition of **jumpHurdle**.

```
void Racer :: jumpUp()
{
        turnLeft();
        move();
        turnRight();
}
```

and

```
void Racer :: glideDown()
{
        turnRight();
        move();
        turnLeft();
}
```

To verify that these instructions are correct, complete and assemble the program. Then simulate a racer robot running the race in Figure 4–2.

## 4.5  NESTED IF INSTRUCTIONS

Although we have seen many IF instructions, we have ignored an entire class of complex IFs. These are known as nested IF instructions, because they are written with an IF instruction nested inside the THEN or ELSE clause of another IF. No new execution rules are needed to simulate nested IFs, but a close adherence to the established rules is required. Simulating nested IF instructions is sometimes difficult because it is easy for us to lose track of where we are in the instruction. The following discussion should be read carefully and understood completely as an example of how to test instructions that include nested IFs.

To demonstrate a nested IF instruction, we propose a task that redistributes beepers in a field. This task requires that a robot named Karel traverse a field and leave exactly one beeper on each corner. The robot must plant a beeper on each barren corner and remove one beeper from every corner where two beepers are present. All corners in this task are constrained to have zero, one, or two beepers on them. One sample initial and final situation are displayed in Figure 4–3. In these situations, multiple beepers on a corner are represented by a number. We can assume that Karel has enough beepers in its beeper-bag to replant the necessary number of corners.

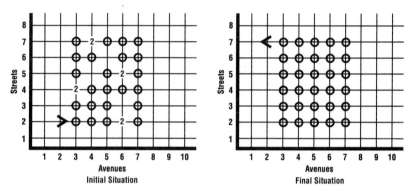

**Figure 4–3**  A Beeper-Replanting Task

The heart of the program that solves this task is an instruction that enables Karel to satisfy the one-beeper requirement for each corner. Following is the instruction. We can provide an override instruction for the **harvestCorner** instruction of the **Harvester** class.

```
void Replanter :: harvestCorner()
{
        if ( ! nextToABeeper() )
        {
                putBeeper();
        }
        else
        {
                pickBeeper();
                if ( ! nextToABeeper() )
                {
                        putBeeper();
                }
        }
}
```

The outer IF statement in this definition is an IF/ELSE and the nested IF statement is an ordinary IF. The nested IF instruction is inside the ELSE clause of the outer IF. Next we simulate Karel in the three possible corner situations: an empty corner, a corner with one beeper, and a corner with two beepers.

In the empty corner situation, Karel executes the outer IF and determines that the test is true. The robot executes the **putBeeper** instruction in the THEN clause, placing one beeper on the corner. Karel has now finished executing the outer IF instruction and thus has finished executing **harvestCorner**.

Next we assume that there is one beeper on Karel's corner. Karel first executes the outer IF. The test is false, so the robot executes the ELSE clause. This clause consists of two instructions: **pickBeeper** and the nested IF instruction. Karel picks the beeper and performs the test associated with the nested IF. The test is true, so Karel executes the THEN clause of this IF instruction and puts a beeper back on the empty corner. Karel is now finished with the nested IF, the ELSE clause, the outer IF, and the entire **harvestCorner** instruction.

Finally, we assume that Karel is on a corner with two beepers. Karel executes the outer IF, finds the test is false, and then executes the ELSE clause. Karel picks up one of the two beepers on the corner. Up to this point Karel has duplicated its actions in the one-beeper situation, but now comes the difference in execution. Karel executes the nested IF instruction, finds the test is false, and skips the nested THEN clause. Once again, Karel is now finished with the nested IF, the ELSE clause, the outer IF, and the entire **harvestCorner** instruction.

It is worth mentioning that when nested IF instructions seem too intricate, we should try replacing the nested IF with a new instruction name. The definition of this auxiliary instruction must command Karel to perform the same actions as the nested IF and may help us better understand what Karel is doing. Because nesting also makes an instruction less readable, a good rule of thumb is to avoid nesting IF instructions more than one level deep. The **harvestCorner** instruction, which has one level of nesting, is rewritten below using an auxiliary instruction.

```
void Replanter :: harvestCorner()
{
        if ( ! nextToABeeper() )
        {
            putBeeper();
        }
        else
        {
            nextToOneReplantOne();
        }
}
```

We write the **nextToOneReplantOne** instruction by copying the ELSE clause from our original definition of **harvestCorner**.

```
void Replanter :: nextToOneReplantOne()
{
        pickBeeper();
        if ( ! nextToABeeper() )
```

```
        {
                putBeeper();
        }
}
```

Given the entire program from Section 3.9 along with either of these new definitions of the **harvestCorner** instruction, do we have a correct solution for the beeper replanting task? We may consider using our old method of verification and test the program with Karel in every possible initial situation, but there are more than 200 trillion[3] different fields that this program must be able to replant correctly. Attempting verification by exhaustively testing Karel in every possible initial situation would be ludicrous.

Instead we will try to establish correctness based on the following informal argument: (1) we have verified that **harvestCorner** works correctly on any corner that is empty or contains one or two beepers, and (2) we can easily verify that our program commands Karel to execute this instruction on each corner of the field. Therefore we conclude that the program correctly replants the entire field.

This argument further enhances the claim that Karel's mechanism for instruction definition is a powerful aid to programming. Usually we can informally conclude that an entire program is correct by verifying that (1) each new instruction in the program works correctly in all possible situations in which it can be executed, and (2) the program executes each new instruction at the appropriate time. This instruction allows us to verify a program by splitting it into separate, simpler verifications, just as stepwise refinement allows us to write a program by splitting it into separate, simpler instructions.

Suppose that a robot is in a situation in which it must determine if there are exactly two beepers on the current corner. We would like to write a predicate to return true if this is so and false otherwise. Suppose that this were needed in some replanting task, so we will add it to the Replanter class. We can write such a predicate if we pick up beepers one at a time and then ask if there are any more. We must remember to put back any beepers that we pick up, however. Note that if we have picked up two beepers, we still need to ask if there are any more to determine whether there are exactly two beepers on the current corner.

```
Boolean Replanter :: exactlyTwoBeepers()
{
        if (nextToABeeper()) // one or more beepers
        {
                pickBeeper();
                if (nextToABeeper())
                // two or more beepers
```

---

[3]There are three different possibilities for each corner, and there are 30 corners in the field. The total number of different fields is thus 3 multiplied by itself 30 times; thus the exact number of different fields is 205,891,132,094,649.

```
                        {
                             pickBeeper();
                             if(nextToABeeper())
                             // more than two
                             {
                                      putBeeper();
                                      putBeeper();
                                      return false;
                             }
                             else // exactly two beepers
                             {
                                      putBeeper();
                                      putBeeper();
                                      return true;
                             }
                        }
                        else // only one beeper
                        {
                                 putBeeper();
                                 return false;
                        }
               }
               else // no beepers
               {
                        return false;
               }
      }
```

## 4.6  MORE COMPLEX TESTS

It is not a trivial matter to have a robot make two or more tests at the same time. More sophisticated programming languages provide the capability to make multiple tests within an IF or an IF/ELSE instruction. We can do this, but we must be clever with our programming, as illustrated by the following example.

Let's assume we are still working on the Lost Beeper Mine problem introduced earlier. Recall that the Lost Beeper Mine is a very large pile of beepers. We have another assignment from that problem—a very important landmark along the way is found where all of the following are true:

- Karel is facing west.
- Karel's right side is blocked.
- Karel's left side is blocked.
- Karel's front is clear.
- There is at least one beeper on the corner.

Following these requirements, we must plan an instruction that will test all of these conditions simultaneously. If we do what seems logical we might try to write something like the following:

```
if ( facingWest()
     AND rightIsBlocked()
     AND leftIsBlocked()
     AND frontIsClear()
     AND nextToABeeper() )
{ . . .
```

This seems logical, but there is one major problem. Robots do not understand AND. The AND will result in a lexical error, so we must use a sequence of nested IF instructions to do the job.

```
if (facingWest() )
{
     if ( ! rightIsClear() )
     {
          if ( ! leftIsClear() )
          {
               if (frontIsClear() )
               {
                    if (nextToABeeper() )
                    {
                         < instruction >
                    }
               }
          }
     }
}
```

If we trace this, we will find that all of the tests must evaluate to true before Karel can execute < instruction >.

Another way to build complex tests is to define new predicates. Suppose we would like to write

```
if (nextToABeeper() AND leftIsBlocked()) { . . .
```

This can be done if we write a new predicate in the class in which we need such a test. For example,

```
Boolean
Prospector :: nextToABeeper_AND_leftIsBlocked()
{
     if(nextToABeeper())
```

```
            {
                  if ( ! leftIsClear())
                  {
                        return true;
                  }
                  else
                  {
                        return false;
                  }
            }
            return false;
      }
```

This can be simplified to:

```
Boolean
Prospector :: nextToABeeper_AND_leftIsBlocked()
{
      if(nextToABeeper())
      {
            return ! leftIsClear();
      }
      return false;
}
```

One way to help determine whether a predicate with two or more conditions is correct is to look at the truth table, which gives all possible combinations of the parts of the predicate. The truth table for AND is shown below.

| nextToABeeper | leftIsBlocked | | AND |
|:---:|:---:|:---:|:---:|
| T | T | \| | T |
| T | F | \| | F |
| F | T | \| | F |
| F | F | \| | F |

The IF instruction in the predicate says that when **nextToABeeper** is true, we should return the negation of **leftIsClear**: the same as **leftIsBlocked**. Note that the first two lines of the truth table also say this. On these two lines **nextToABeeper** is true and the **leftIsBlocked** lines exactly match the AND lines here. Likewise, the predicate says that when **nextToABeeper** is false we should return **false**. Again, this matches the truth table exactly, since on the last two lines, where **nextToABeeper** is false, we return **false**.

Note that in the **nextToABeeper_AND_leftIsBlocked** instruction there is no need to check that the left is clear if we have already determined that we are not next to a beeper. We can simply return false in this case. We only need to check the second part of the AND when the first part is true. This is known as <u>short-circuit evaluation</u> of the predicate, and it is very useful. To use it wisely, however, so that a user isn't misled, you must check the leftmost part (**nextToABeeper**) first. Some computer languages that have the AND operator built into them automatically use short-circuit evaluation. Others do not.

A similar instruction can be used to simulate

```
if (nextToABeeper() OR leftIsBlocked()) { . . .
```

The truth table for an OR is as follows. Notice that when **nextToABeeper** is true the OR is also true, and when **nextToABeeper** is false the result is the same as **leftIsBlocked**.

| nextToABeeper | leftIsBlocked | | OR |
|:---:|:---:|:---:|:---:|
| T | T | &#124; | T |
| T | F | &#124; | T |
| F | T | &#124; | T |
| F | F | &#124; | F |

## 4.7  WHEN TO USE AN IF INSTRUCTION

Thus far we have spent most of our time and effort in this chapter explaining how the IF and the IF/ELSE instructions work. It is at this point that students are usually told, "Write a program that uses the IF and the IF/ELSE instructions so that a robot can ..." It is also at this point that we hear the following question being asked by students: "I understand how these work, but I don't understand when to use them." It is understanding when to use them that is the focus of this section.

Let's review what the IF and the IF/ELSE instructions allow robots to do in a robot program:

- The IF instruction allows a robot to decide whether to execute or skip entirely the block of instructions within the THEN clause.

- The IF/ELSE instruction allows a robot to decide whether to execute the block of instructions in the THEN clause or the ELSE clause.

- Nesting these instructions allows Karel to make more complex choices if required.

We can use these three statements to build a decision map. A decision map is a technique that asks questions about the problem we are trying to solve. The answers to the questions determine the branch we follow through the map. Figure 4–4 is the section of the decision map that a programmer would use for choosing between an IF and an IF/ELSE.

To use this part of the decision map we must be at a point during our implementation where a robot needs to choose from among alternatives. We use the map by asking each question as we encounter it and following the path that has the answer. If this is done correctly, we eventually arrive at an implementation suggestion. If the map does not work, we probably do not need to choose between alternatives or have

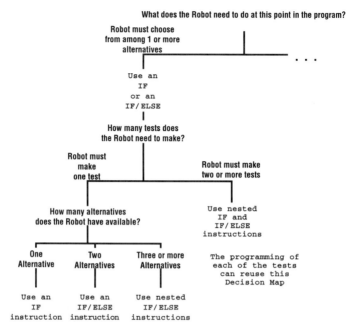

**Figure 4–4**   Part of the Decision Map

not correctly thought out our plan. By the way, we say we choose from among one alternative as a shorthand for the situation where the choice is simply to do something or not.

Suppose a robot must face north if there is a beeper on the current corner and face south otherwise. How many tests does the robot have to make? One—either **nextToABeeper** or **!nextToABeeper**. This answer directs us down the left path to the next question: How many alternatives does the robot have available? Two—the robot must either face north or face south. This takes us down the path to the IF/ELSE instruction. Our implementation looks like this:

```
if( nextToABeeper() )
{
        faceNorth();
}
else
{
        faceSouth();
}
```

## 4.8   TRANSFORMATIONS FOR SIMPLIFYING IF INSTRUCTIONS

This section discusses four useful transformations that help simplify programs containing IF instructions. We start by observing that when two program fragments result in a robot's performing exactly the same actions, we call this pair of fragments execution equivalent. For a simple example, `turnLeft(); putBeeper();` is execution equivalent to `putBeeper(); turnLeft();`.

In general, we can create one execution equivalent IF/ELSE instruction from another by replacing < test > with its opposite and interchanging the THEN and the ELSE clauses as illustrated below. We call this transformation test reversal. Notice that if we perform test reversal twice on the same instruction, we get back to the instruction with which we started.

```
if(frontIsClear())              if( ! frontIsClear() )
{                               {
      move();                          jumpHurdle();
}                               }
else                            else
{                               {
      jumpHurdle();                    move();
}                               }
```

Test reversal can be used to help novice programmers overcome the following difficulty. Suppose that we start to write an IF instruction and get ourselves into the dilemma illustrated below on the left. The problem is that we want a robot to do nothing special when its front is clear,[4] but when its front is blocked we want Karel to execute < instruction >. We would like to remove the THEN clause, but doing so would cause a syntax error—Karel does not understand an IF/ELSE instruction without a THEN clause. The solution to our problem is illustrated on the right.

```
if(frontIsClear())              if( ! frontIsClear())
{                               {
      doNothing();                     < instruction >
}                               }
else
{
      <instruction>
}
```

To transform the IF on the left into the IF on the right, we use test reversal. First we change < test > to its opposite, and then switch the `doNothing` instruction into the ELSE clause and bring < instruction > into the THEN clause. By the previous discussion of test reversal, execution equivalence is preserved. Finally, the new ELSE clause (which contains the `doNothing` instruction) can be removed, resulting in the simpler IF instruction on the right.

---

[4]We can define the instruction `doNothing` as four left turns. Executing this instruction would leave Karel's position unchanged, and this instruction is also immune to error shutoffs. This would be wasteful of the Robot's battery capacity, however. We could also simply not write anything between the braces of the THEN part.

The second transformation we discuss is <u>bottom factoring</u>. Bottom factoring is illustrated below, where we will show that the IF/ELSE instruction on the left is execution equivalent to the program fragment on the right. We have kept the bracketed words in these instructions because their exact replacements do not affect this transformation.

```
if(<test> )                        if(<test> )
{                                  {
        <instruction_1>                    <instruction_1>
        <instruction_3>            }
}                                  else
else                               {
{                                          <instruction_2>
        <instruction_2>            }
        <instruction_3>            <instruction_3>
}
```

In the program fragment on the right, we have factored $<$ instruction_3 $>$ out of the bottom of each clause in the IF. We justify the correctness of this transformation as follows: If $<$ test $>$ is true, the instruction on the left has the robot execute $<$ instruction_1 $>$ directly followed by $<$ instruction_3 $>$. In the program fragment on the right, if $<$ test $>$ is true the robot executes $<$ instruction_1 $>$ and then, having finished the IF, it executes $<$ instruction_3 $>$. Thus, when $<$ test $>$ is true, these forms are execution equivalent. A similar argument holds between the left and right fragments whenever $<$ test $>$ is false.

In summary, $<$ instruction_3 $>$ is executed in the IF on the left regardless of whether $<$ test $>$ is true or false. So we might as well remove it from each clause and put it directly after the entire IF/ELSE instruction. Moreover, if the bottoms of each clause were larger but still identical, we could bottom factor all of the common instructions and still preserve execution equivalence. Think of this process as bottom factoring one instruction at a time until all common instructions have been factored. Since execution equivalence is preserved during each factoring step, the resulting program fragment is execution equivalent to the original instruction.

The third transformation we discuss in this section is <u>top factoring</u>. Although this transformation may seem as simple and easy to use as bottom factoring, we will see that not all instructions can be top factored successfully. We divide our discussion of this transformation into three parts. First, we examine an instruction that can safely be top factored. Then we show an instruction that cannot be top factored successfully. Finally, we state a general rule that tells us which IF instructions can safely be top factored.

Top factoring can safely be used in the following example to convert the instruction on the left into the simpler program fragment on the right. These two forms can be shown to be execution equivalent by a justification similar to the one used in our discussion of bottom factoring.

```
if(facingNorth())               move();
{                               if(facingNorth())
        move();                 {
        turnLeft();                     turnLeft();
}                               }
else                            else
{                               {
        move();                         turnRight();
        turnRight();            }
}
```

In the next example, we have incorrectly used the top factoring transformation. We will discover that the program fragment on the right is not execution equivalent to the instruction on the left.

```
if(nextToABeeper())             move();
{                               if(nextToABeeper())
        move();                 {
        turnLeft();                     turnLeft();
}                               }
else                            else
{                               {
        move();                         turnRight();
        turnRight();            }
}
```

To show that these forms execute differently, let's assume that a robot named Karel is on a corner containing one beeper, and that the corner in front of the robot is barren. If Karel executes the instruction on the left, the robot will first find that it is next to a beeper, and then it will execute the THEN clause of the IF by moving forward and turning to its left. The program fragment on the right will first move Karel forward to the next corner and then will instruct it to test for a beeper. Because this new corner does not contain a beeper, Karel will execute the ELSE clause of the IF, which causes the robot to turn to its right. Thus top factoring in this example does not preserve execution equivalence.

Why can we correctly use top factoring in the first example but not in the second? The first instruction can be top factored safely because the test that determines which way Karel is facing is not changed by having it move forward. Therefore, whether Karel moves first or not, the evaluation of the test will remain unchanged. But in the second example the move changes the corner on which Karel checks for a beeper, so the robot is not performing the test under the same conditions. The general rule is that we may top factor an instruction only when the conditions under which the test is performed do not change between the original and factored versions of the instruction.

The fourth and final transformation is used to remove redundant tests in nested IF instructions. We call this transformation <u>redundant-test factoring</u> and show one application of this rule.

```
if(facingWest())                  if(facingWest())
{                                 {
      move();                           move();
      if(facingWest())                  turnLeft();
      {                           }
            turnLeft();
      }
}
```

In the instruction on the left, there is no need for the nested IF instruction to recheck the condition **facingWest**. The THEN clause of the outer IF is executed only if Karel is facing west, and the move inside the THEN clause does not normally change the direction that Karel is facing. Therefore **facingWest** is always true when Karel executes this nested IF instruction. This argument shows that Karel always executes the THEN clause of this nested IF. So the entire nested IF instruction can be replaced by **turnLeft**, as has been done in the instruction on the right. Once again, this transformation preserves execution equivalence. Of course, if we have given **move** a new meaning in the class of which this is a member, then we cannot guarantee that **move** doesn't change the direction. In this case the two fragments would not be equivalent. A similar transformation applies whenever we look for a redundant test in an ELSE clause. Remember, though, in an ELSE clause < test > is false.

This transformation is also a bit more subtle than bottom factoring, and we must be careful when trying to use it. The potential difficulty is that intervening instructions might change Karel's position in an unknown way. For example, if instead of the **move** instruction we had used a **turnAroundIfNextToABeeper** instruction, we could not have used redundant-test factoring. Here we cannot be sure whether Karel would be facing west or east when it had to execute the nested IF.

These four transformations can help us make our programs smaller, simpler, more logical, and, most important, more readable.

## 4.9   PROBLEM SET

The problems in this section require the use of the IF instruction in its two forms. Try using stepwise refinement on these problems, but no matter what instruction you use to obtain a solution, write a clear and understandable program. Keep the nesting level small for those problems requiring nested IF instructions. Use proper punctuation and grammar, especially within the THEN and ELSE clauses of the IF instructions. Carefully simulate each definition and program that you write to ensure that there are no execution or intent errors.

1. Write a new predicate `leftIsBlocked` that determines whether there is a wall exactly one-half block away on a robot's left. Be sure that when it terminates, the robot is on the same corner and facing in the same direction.

2. Look at the following instruction. Is there a simpler, execution-equivalent instruction? If so, write it down; if not, explain why. *Hint:* A simplifying transformation for the IF may prove useful. Common sense helps, too.

```
if( ! nextToABeeper())
{
        move();
}
else
{
        move();
}
```

3. Assume that a Prospector robot is on a corner with either one or two beepers. Write a new instruction that commands the robot to face north if it is started on a corner with one beeper and to face south if it is started on a corner with two beepers. Besides facing the robot in the required direction, after it has executed this instruction there must be no beepers left on the corner. Name this instruction `findNextDirection`.

4. Write another version of `findNextDirection` (see the previous problem). In this version the robot must eventually face the same direction, but it also must leave the same number of beepers on the corner as were there originally.

5. Write an instruction that turns a robot off if the robot is completely surrounded by walls, unable to move in any direction. If the robot is not surrounded, it should execute this instruction by leaving itself turned on and by remaining on the same corner, facing the same direction in which it started. Name this instruction `turnOffIfSurrounded`. *Hint:* To write this instruction correctly, you will need to include a `turnOff` inside it. This combination is perfectly legal, but it is the first time that you will use a `turnOff` instruction outside the main task block.

6. Program a robot to run a mile-long steeplechase. The steeplechase course is similar to the hurdle race, but here the barriers can be one, two, or three blocks high. Figure 4–5 shows one sample initial situation, where the robot's final situation and path are shown on the right. Call the class of this new robot `Steeplechaser`. It should have `Racer` as a parent class. Override appropriate instructions of `Racer` to implement the new behavior.

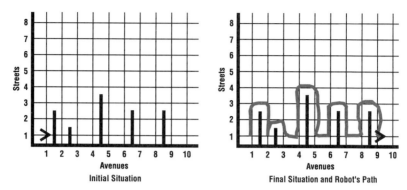

**Figure 4–5**   Steeplechase Race Task

7. Rewrite and check the following new instruction, taking care to interpret all of the robot programming grammar rules correctly. This instruction uses nested IFs to face a robot toward the east; verify that it is correct by simulation. *Hint:* When trying to check this instruction, ignore the instruction indentation. One way of doing this is to have someone read you the instruction. While they are reading the instruction, you should keep track of the meaningful components of the instruction. This is exactly what the factory does when it reads instructions to robots at the factory.

```
void Prospector ::  faceEast()
{
      if(not_facingEast())
{
            if(facingWest()) {
                  turnLeft();
                  turnLeft(); }
      else
            { if(facingNorth())
{
                  turnRight(); }
            else  {
                  turnLeft();
                  }
            }
      }
}
```

8.  The current version of **mysteryInstruction** is syntactically correct but very difficult to read. Simplify it by using the IF transformations.

```
void Prospector ::  mysteryInstruction()
{
      if(facingWest())
    {
        move();
        turnRight();
        if(facingNorth())
        {
              move();
        }
        turnAround();
    }
    else
    {
        move();
        turnLeft();
        move();
        turnAround();
    }
}
```

9.  Write an instruction **followWallRight** for the **Maze_Walker** class, assuming that whenever a robot executes this instruction there is a wall directly to the right. Figure 4–6 shows four of the different position changes that the robot must be able to make. This instruction is the cornerstone for a program that directs a robot to escape from a maze (this maze-escape problem is Problem 17 in Section 5.9).

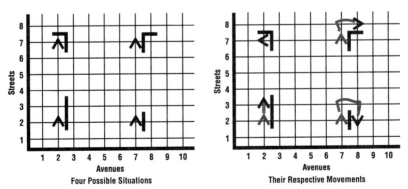

**Figure 4–6**   The **followWallRight** Specification

10.  Program a robot to run a mile-long steeplechase in which the fences are made from beepers instead of wall segments. The robot must jump the fences in this race by picking up the beepers that make up the fences. Each fence is made from beepers that are positioned in columns that are one, two, or three blocks long. Corners have either zero or one beeper. There are no gaps in any of the fences. Figure 4–7 shows one sample initial situation.

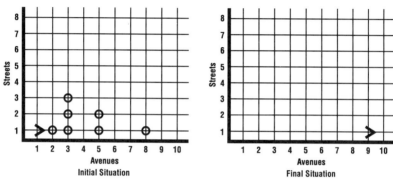

**Figure 4–7**   Different Steeplechase

11.  A robot named Karel has been hired to carpet some "small rooms" along a one-mile section of its world. A small room is a corner that has a wall segment immediately to the west, north, and east. The door is to the south. Karel is to put a single beeper in only the small rooms and on no other corners. Figure 4–8 shows one set of initial and final situations. You may assume that Karel has exactly eight beepers in its beeper-bag.

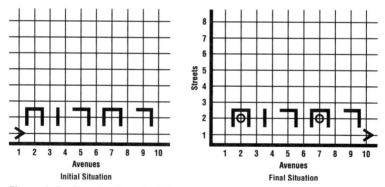

**Figure 4–8**   Carpeting Some Small Rooms

**12.** Karel did so well on the job in Problem 11 that the robot has been hired for a more complex carpeting task. The area to be carpeted is still one mile long. The rooms are now one, two, or three blocks long. The room must have continuous walls on its west and east sides and at its northern end. If any walls are missing, the area must not be carpeted. Also, Karel must not reuse beepers. This means that once a beeper has been put down, it must not be picked up. Figure 4–9 shows one set of initial and final situations. You give Karel exactly 24 beepers during construction and delivery.

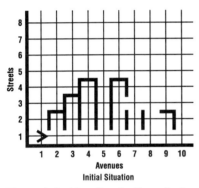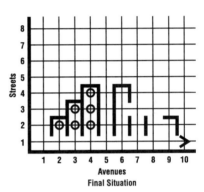

**Figure 4–9** More Complex Carpet Laying

**13.** Write a predicate that will return true if and only if the robot executing it both next to a beeper AND its left is blocked. Write another predicate that will return true if the robot executing it is either next to a beeper OR its left is blocked. In this latter case, if the robot is next to a beeper with its left blocked, it should also return true. Recall that nested IFs can be used to implement AND. Similarly, a sequence of IFs can be used to implement OR. What general conclusions can you draw from this exercise?

**14.** Write a predicate that will return true if and only if the robot executing it has exactly two beepers in its beeper-bag. Can we write a predicate that will return true if and only if the robot executing it is on a corner with exactly two other robots? Why or why not? Write another predicate that will return true if and only if the robot executing it is on a corner with at most two beepers.

# 5 INSTRUCTIONS THAT REPEAT

This chapter completes our discussion of the instructions built into the robot programming language vocabulary. The two new instructions we will learn are LOOP and WHILE. Both instructions can repeatedly execute any instruction that a robot understands, including nested LOOP and WHILE instructions. These additions greatly enhance the conciseness and power of the robot programming language. In Section 5.7 we will construct a complex robot program by using stepwise refinement and all of the instructions we have learned.

Since we are becoming experienced robot programmers, an abbreviated view of the robot world will be used for some figures. To reduce visual clutter, the street and avenue labels and, occasionally, the southern or western boundary walls will not be shown. As usual, our examples will use a single robot, often named Karel. Since most of our examples will involve manipulation of beepers, we suppose that we are building a class named `Beeper_Controller`.

## 5.1 THE LOOP INSTRUCTION

When we program a robot, having it repeat an instruction a certain number of times is sometimes necessary. We previously handled this problem by writing the instruction as many times as needed. The LOOP instruction gives us a mechanism that allows Karel to repeat another instruction a specified number of times. It has the following general form:

```
loop  (<positive-number> )
{
        <instruction-list>
}
```

This instruction introduces the reserved word `loop`. The bracketed word <positive-number> tells the robot how many times to execute the instruction list that replaces <instruction-list>. We refer to <instruction-list> as the <u>body</u> of the LOOP instruction. This instruction is called LOOP because one can imagine the instructions of the <instruction-list> arranged in a circle. If we execute them one after the other, we will come to the first one just after the last one. Our first example of a LOOP instruction is an alternative definition of `turnRight`.

```
void Beeper_Controller:: turnRight()
{
    loop (3)
    {
        turnLeft();
    }
}
```

As a second example, we rewrite the `harvestOneRow` instruction that was written in Section 3.8.3. This definition originally comprised nine primitive instructions, but by using LOOP we can define the instruction more concisely. With this new, more general version of `harvestOneRow`, we can now easily increase or decrease the number of beepers harvested per row; all we need to change is <positive-number> in the LOOP instruction.

```
void Harvester :: harvestOneRow()
{
    harvestCorner();
    loop (4)
    {
        move();
        harvestCorner();
    }
}
```

Remember that the robot is originally on a corner with a beeper, so we need to harvest the first corner before we move. This is equivalent to the following version, however. In this version we must remember to harvest the last corner after the loop completes, since we ended with a move and have harvested only the first four corners in this row.

```
void Harvester :: harvestOneRow()
{
    loop (4)
    {
        harvestCorner();
        move();
    }
    harvestCorner();
}
```

Finally, we show one LOOP instruction nested within another. Carefully observe the way that the inner loop both begins and ends within the outer loop.

```
void Beeper_Controller :: walkSquareOfLength_6()
{
      loop (4)
      {
            loop (6)
            {
                  move();
            }
            turnLeft();
      }
}
```

If we assume no intervening walls, this instruction moves the robot around the perimeter of a square whose sides are six blocks long. The outer LOOP instruction loops a total of four times, once for each side of the square. Each time the outer LOOP's body is executed, the robot executes two instructions. First the robot executes the nested LOOP, which moves it six blocks. Then it executes the **turnLeft**, which prepares it to trace the next side. Thus the robot executes a total of 24 moves and four left turns, which are arranged in an order that makes it travel in a square.

## 5.2   THE WHILE INSTRUCTION

In this section we explain the WHILE instruction and analyze many of its interesting properties. It is the most powerful instruction that is built into the robot vocabulary.

### 5.2.1   Why WHILE is Needed

To motivate the need for a WHILE instruction, we look at what should be a simple programming task. Assume that a robot is initially facing east on some street, and somewhere east of it on that same street is a beeper. The robot's task is to move forward until it is on the same corner as the beeper and then pick it up. Despite this simple description, the program is impossible to write with our current repertoire of instructions.[1] Two attempts at solving this problem might be written as follows.

```
if ( ! nextToABeeper())              loop ( ? )
{                                    {
      move;                                move();
```

---

[1]We could also use the technique called <u>recursion</u>, which is discussed in Chapter 6.

```
}                                              }
if ( ! nextToABeeper())           pickBeeper();
{
        move();
}

                    .

                    .

                    .

if ( ! nextToABeeper())
{
            move();
}
pickBeeper();
```

We can interpret what is meant by these instructions, but robots understand neither "..." nor "?". The difficulty is that we do not know in advance how many move instructions the robot must execute before it arrives at the same corner as the beeper; we do not even have a guaranteed upper limit. The beeper may be on the robot's starting street corner, or it may be a million blocks away. The robot must be able to accomplish this task without knowing in advance the number of corners that it will pass before reaching the beeper. We must program our robot to execute move instructions repeatedly until it senses that it is next to the beeper. What we need is an instruction that combines the repetition ability of the LOOP instruction with the testing ability of the IF instruction.

## 5.2.2  The Form of the WHILE Instruction

The WHILE instruction commands a robot to repeat another instruction as long as some test remains true. The WHILE instruction is executed somewhat similarly to an IF instruction, except that the WHILE instruction repeatedly executes itself as long as <test> is true. The general form of the WHILE instruction is as follows:

```
while (<test> )
{
        <instruction-list>
}
```

The new reserved word **while** starts this instruction, the parentheses enclose <test>, and braces enclose the <instruction-list> in the usual way. The conditions that can replace <test> are the same ones used in the IF instructions.

A robot executes a WHILE loop by first checking <test> in its current situation. If <test> is true, the robot executes <instruction-list> and then reexecutes the entire WHILE loop. If <test> is false, the robot is finished with the WHILE instruction, and it continues by executing the instructions following the entire WHILE loop. Here is a sample WHILE instruction that solves the problem that began this discussion:

```
void Beeper_Controller :: goToBeeper()
{
      while ( ! nextToABeeper())
      {
            move();
      }
}
```

This instruction moves a robot forward as long as **nextToABeeper** is false. When the robot is finally next to a beeper, it finishes executing the WHILE loop. The following instruction is another simple example of a WHILE loop, and we will examine its behavior in detail.

```
void Beeper_Controller :: clearCornerOfBeepers()
{
      while ( nextToABeeper() )
      {
            pickBeeper();
      }
}
```

Suppose we have a robot named Karel in class **Beeper_Controller** and send it the message **Karel.clearCornerOfBeepers**. This instruction commands Karel to pick up all of the beepers on a corner. Let's simulate Karel's execution of this instruction on a corner containing two beepers. Karel first determines whether **nextToABeeper** is true or false. Finding the test true, it executes the body of the WHILE loop, which is the **pickBeeper** instruction. Karel then reexecutes the entire WHILE loop. The robot finds <test> is true (one beeper is still left) and executes the body of the WHILE loop. After picking up the second beeper, Karel reexecutes the entire WHILE instruction. Although we know that no beepers are remaining, Karel is unaware of this fact until it rechecks the WHILE loop test. Now Karel rechecks the test and discovers that **nextToABeeper** is false, so the robot is finished executing the WHILE loop. Because the entire definition consists of one WHILE loop, Karel is finished executing **clearCornerOfBeepers**. It appears that no matter how many beepers are initially on the corner, Karel will eventually pick them all up when this instruction is executed.

But what happens if Karel executes **clearCornerOfBeepers** on a corner that has no beepers? In this situation, <test> is false the first time that the WHILE instruction is executed, so the loop body is not executed at all. Therefore Karel also handles this situation correctly. The key fact to remember about a WHILE instruction is that until Karel discovers that <test> has become false—and it may be false the first time—Karel repeatedly checks <test> and executes the loop's body.

### 5.2.3 Building a WHILE Loop—The Four-Step Process

In the previous chapter on IFs we discussed the problems novice programmers frequently face when introduced to a new programming construct. We are in a similar situation with the WHILE loop. We have seen the form of a WHILE loop, looked at an example, and traced the execution of the example. Before using a WHILE loop in a robot program, it would be helpful to have a framework for thinking about the WHILE loop.

We should consider using a WHILE loop only when a robot must do something an unknown number of times. If we are faced with such a situation, we can build our WHILE loop by following the four-step process shown below. To illustrate these steps, we will again use the problem of having a robot named Karel pick all beepers from a corner without knowing the initial number of beepers on the corner.

> *Step 1.* Identify the one test that must be true when Karel is finished with the loop.

In the problem, Karel must pick all beepers on the corner. If we consider only tests that involve beepers, we have four to choose from: **anyBeepersInBeeperBag**, **nextToABeeper**, and their opposites. Which one is the test we want? When Karel is finished, there should be no beepers left on the corner, so the test we want to be true is

```
! nextToABeeper().
```

> *Step 2.* Use the opposite form of the test identified in step 1 as the loop <test>.

This implies that we should use **nextToABeeper**. Does this make sense? The WHILE instruction continues to execute the loop body as long as the test is true and stops when it is false. As long as Karel is next to a beeper Karel should pick it up. When Karel is done, there will be no beepers on the corner.

> *Step 3.* Within the WHILE, make progress toward completion of the WHILE. We need to do something within the WHILE to ensure that the test eventually evaluates to false so that the WHILE loop stops. Often it is helpful to do the minimum amount of work that is necessary to advance toward the completion of the task.

Something within the body of the loop must allow the test to eventually evaluate to false or the loop will run forever. This implies that there must be some instruction (or sequence of instructions) within the loop that is related to the test. In this problem, what must be done to bring us closer to the test being false? Since we are testing for **nextToABeeper**, we must pick one (and only one) beeper somewhere in the loop. We can argue that if Karel keeps picking one beeper, it must eventually pick all the beepers, leaving none on the corner. Why pick only one beeper during each iteration? Why not two or three? If there is only one beeper on the corner, and we instruct Karel to pick up more than one, an error shutoff will occur. Picking just one beeper during each iteration of the loop is the minimum needed to guarantee that all the beepers are eventually picked up.

***Step 4.*** Do whatever is required before or after the WHILE instruction is executed to ensure that we solve the given problem.

In this example, we have to do nothing before or after the loop. However, there are times when we may miss one iteration of the loop and have to "clean things up," which can be done either before or after the WHILE. Also, we sometimes need to execute an instruction or two before the WHILE loop to get our robot into the correct position.

If we follow these four steps carefully, we reduce the chance of having intent errors and infinite repetition when we test our program. Infinite execution is the error that occurs when we begin to execute a WHILE instruction, but it never terminates. This is discussed in Section 5.3.2.


## 5.2.4  A More Interesting Problem

Let's apply the steps just presented to a new problem. A robot named Karel is somewhere in the world facing south. One beeper is on each corner between Karel's current position and the southern boundary wall. There is no beeper on the corner on which Karel is currently standing. (See Figure 5-1.) Write a new instruction, `clearAllBeepersToTheWall`, to pick all of the beepers.

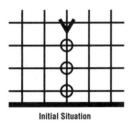

**Initial Situation**

**Figure    5-1**  Pick All
Beepers

As before, let's ask ourselves some questions:

**Question:**  What do we know about Karel's initial situation?

**Answer:**  Karel is facing south.
Karel is an unknown distance from the southern boundary wall.
Each corner between Karel and the southern boundary wall has one beeper.

**Question:**  Does any of this information provide insight toward a solution?

**Answer:**  Karel can travel forward until it reaches the southern boundary wall.
It can pick a beeper from each corner as it travels.

We have the beginnings of a plan. The process continues as follows:

**Question:**  What robot instruction can we use to keep Karel traveling southward until it reaches the southern boundary wall?

**Answer:**    Since traveling to the southern boundary wall requires an unknown number of move instructions, we can use a WHILE loop.

**Question:**  How do we actually use the WHILE loop?

**Answer:**    We can use the four-step process as follows:

*Step 1.*   Identify the one test that must be true when Karel is finished with the loop. Karel will be at the southern boundary wall, so the test, `frontIsClear`, will be false, so ! `frontIsClear` will be true.

*Step 2.*   Use the opposite form of the test identified in step 1 as the loop <test>. `frontIsClear` is the opposite form.

*Step 3.*   Do the minimum needed to ensure that the test eventually evaluates to false so that the WHILE loop stops. Karel must move forward one block within the loop body, but we must be careful here. Karel is not yet standing on a beeper, so it must move first before picking the beeper. We can use a single `pickBeeper` instruction because there is only one beeper on each corner.

*Step 4.*   Do whatever is required before or after the WHILE is executed to ensure that we solve the given problem. Since Karel is already facing south, we do not have to do anything.

Based on this discussion we can write the following new instruction:

```
void Beeper_Controller :: clearAllBeepersToTheWall()
{
     while ( frontIsClear())
     {
          move();
          pickBeeper();
     }
}
```

Our work is not finished. We must carefully trace the execution before we certify it as correct. Can we test all possible situations that Karel could start this task in? No. We cannot test all possible situations, but we can test several and do a reasonable job of convincing ourselves that the instruction is correct. One method of informally reasoning about the instruction follows.

*First.*    Show that the instruction works correctly when the initial situation results in the test being false. That would mean that the initial situation would look like Figure 5-2.

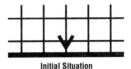

**Initial Situation**

**Figure 5-2** The Same
Task Without Beepers

**Second.** We must show that each time the loop body is executed, Karel's new situation is a simpler and similar version of the old situation. By simpler we mean that Karel now has less work to do before finishing the loop. By similar we mean that Karel's situation has not radically changed during its execution of the loop body (in this example a nonsimilar change could mean that Karel is facing a different direction). If our new instruction is correct, we should see the changes in Figure 5-3.

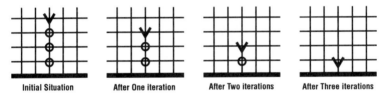

| Initial Situation | After One iteration | After Two iterations | After Three iterations |

**Figure 5-3** Tracing Karel's Progress Executing the Loop

After each iteration of the loop, the current corner should have no beepers. Trace the robot's execution of the loop and verify that it is correct.

## 5.3 ERRORS TO AVOID WITH WHILE LOOPS

The WHILE loop provides a powerful tool for our robot programs. Using it wisely, we can instruct robots to solve some very complex problems. However, the sharper the ax, the deeper it can cut. With the power of the WHILE loop comes the potential for making some powerful mistakes. This section will examine several typical errors that can be made when using the WHILE loop. If we are aware of these errors, we will have a better chance of avoiding them or, at least, an easier time identifying them for correction.

### 5.3.1 The Fence Post Problem

If we order five fence sections, how many fence posts do we need? The obvious answer is five! But it is wrong. Look at Figure 5-4.

The figure should help us to understand why the correct answer is six. We can encounter the fence post problem when using the WHILE loop. Let's take the previous problem with a slight twist and put a beeper on Karel's starting corner. (See Figure 5-5.)

**Figure 5-4**    The Fence Post Problem

Since this is a slight modification of the **clearAllBeepersToTheWall** task of the class **Beeper_Controller**, it would be advantageous to have solutions to both problems available. One good way to do this is to build a new class, say **Beeper_Sweeper**, derived from **Beeper_Controller**, in which to implement this new instruction, which is just an override of **clearAllBeepersToTheWall**.

Suppose we decide to solve this problem by reversing the order of the instructions in the original loop body and have Karel pick the beeper before moving:

```
void Beeper_Sweeper :: clearAllBeepersToTheWall()
{
    while ( frontIsClear() )
    {
        pickBeeper();
        move();
    }
}
```

If we trace the instruction's execution carefully, we will discover that the loop still finishes; there is no error shutoff. However, the southernmost beeper is not picked. (See Figure 5-6.)

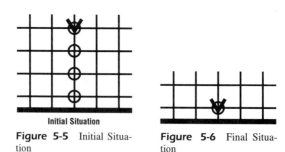

**Figure 5-5**  Initial Situation

**Figure 5-6**  Final Situation

In this example the beepers were the fence posts and the moves were the fence sections. The WHILE loop executes the same number of **pickBeeper** and **move** instructions. Consequently, there will be one beeper left when the loop finishes. This is where step 4 in the four-step process comes in. We now have a situation where we must do something before or after the loop to make sure we solve the given problem. There are at least two ways to handle this. Here is one:

```
void Beeper_Sweeper :: clearAllBeepersToTheWall()
{
    while ( frontIsClear() )
    {
        pickBeeper();
        move();
    }
    pickBeeper();
}
```

Our solution is simply to pick the final beeper after the WHILE loop stops executing. What is the other way to solve this fence post problem? We could pick up the beeper on the start corner first. This would put us in the initial position of **Beeper_Controller :: clearAllBeepersToTheWall**. This means that we can actually use that instruction to write this one.

```
void Beeper_Sweeper :: clearAllBeepersToTheWall()
{
    pickBeeper();
    Beeper_Controller :: clearAllBeepersToTheWall();
}
```

## 5.3.2   Infinite Execution

Having looked at step 4 in the four-step process, let's now refocus our attention on step 3: Do what is needed to ensure that the test eventually evaluates to false so that the WHILE loop stops. Sometimes we forget to include an instruction (or sequence of instructions) the execution of which allows the test eventually to become false. Here is an example:

```
while ( facingNorth() )
{
    pickBeeper();
    move();
}
```

Look at this loop carefully. Is there any instruction within the loop body that will change the robot's direction? Neither **pickBeeper** nor **move** does so. The loop will iterate zero times if the robot is initially facing any direction other than north. Unfortunately, if it is facing north we condemn the robot to walk forever (since the world is infinite to the north) or to execute an error shutoff if it arrives at a corner without a beeper.[2] We must be very careful when we plan the body of the WHILE loop to avoid the possibility of infinite repetition.

### 5.3.3 When the Test of a WHILE is Checked

Section 5.2.2 explained how a robot executes a WHILE instruction, yet unless the instruction is read carefully, there may be some ambiguity. In this section we closely examine the execution of a WHILE instruction and explain a common misconception about when a robot checks <test>. Examine the following instruction carefully.

```
void Beeper_Controller :: harvestLine()
{
    while ( nextToABeeper() )
    {
        pickBeeper();
        move();
    }
}
```

This instruction commands a robot to pick up a line of beepers. The robot finishes executing this instruction after moving one block beyond the final corner that has a beeper.

Let's simulate this new instruction in detail for a line of two beepers. The robot is again named Karel. Karel starts its task on the same corner as the first beeper. Karel executes the WHILE instruction and finds that the test is true, so it executes the body of the loop. The loop body instructs Karel to pick up the beeper and then move to the next corner. Now Karel reexecutes the loop; the test is checked, and again Karel senses that it is next to a beeper. The robot picks up the second beeper and moves forward. Karel then executes the loop again. Now when the test is checked, the robot finds that its corner is beeperless, so it is finished executing the WHILE loop. The definition of **harvestLine** contains only one instruction—this WHILE loop—so **harvestLine** is also finished.

The point demonstrated here is that Karel checks <test> only before it executes the body of the loop. Karel is totally insensitive to <test> while executing instructions that are inside the loop body. A common misconception among novice programmers is that Karel checks <test> after each instruction is executed inside the loop body. This is an incorrect interpretation of when Karel checks <test>.

Let's see what would happen if Karel used the incorrect interpretation to execute the **harvestLine** instruction in the two-beeper situation. This interpretation would force Karel to finish the WHILE loop as soon as it was not next to a beeper. Karel would start by determining whether it were next to a beeper. Finding the test true, Karel would execute the loop body. This is fine so far, but after executing

---

[2]Of course, if we have overridden **pickBeeper** or **move**, then anything is possible. One of the new versions could change the direction, and then the robot would exit the WHILE.

the `pickBeeper`, Karel would not be next to a beeper anymore. So, according to this incorrect interpretation, Karel would now be finished with the loop and would be limited to picking up only one beeper regardless of the length of the beeper line.

Recall again the fence sections and fence posts. Notice that the body of a WHILE is like a fence section and the test is like a fence post. The number of test evaluations is always one more than the number of executions of the body of the WHILE instruction.

## 5.4   NESTED WHILE LOOPS

We have already discussed nesting, or the placing of one instruction within a similar instruction. Nesting WHILE loops can be a very useful technique if done properly, and in this section we look at both a good and a bad example of nesting.

### 5.4.1   A Good Example of Nesting

We will use a modification of a previous problem. A robot named Karel is somewhere in the world facing south. Between its current location and the southern boundary wall are beepers. We do not know how many beepers are on each corner (some corners may even have no beepers). Write a new instruction that will direct Karel to pick all the beepers between its current location and the southern boundary wall. (See Figure 5-7.)

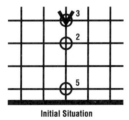

**Initial Situation**

**Figure 5-7**   A Problem to Move and Pick Beepers

We can use our question-and-answer format to plan a solution to this problem.

**Question:**   What is the problem?

**Answer:**   We must move Karel an unknown distance and have Karel pick an unknown number of beepers from each corner it passes.

**Question:**   What does Karel have to do?

**Answer:**   Karel must perform two tasks:

- First, Karel must walk an unknown distance to the southern wall.
- Second, Karel must pick all the beepers on each corner it encounters. There may be from zero to a very large number of beepers on each corner.

Let's concentrate on the first task and save the second task for later.

**Question:** What instruction can we use to keep Karel moving forward to the southern boundary wall?

**Answer:** Since this requires an unknown number of iterations of the **move** instruction, we can use the WHILE loop.

We can apply the four-step process for building WHILE loops and write the following code for Karel to test.

```
while ( frontIsClear() )
{
        move();
}
```

If Karel executes this instruction correctly, then our plan is on the right track. However, if Karel stops before arriving at the boundary wall or executes an error shutoff when it tries to move through the wall, we must reanalyze our plan. This instruction works properly, so we now consider the second task: the picking of all beepers on each corner Karel encounters as it travels to the boundary wall.

**Question:** What instruction will allow Karel to pick all the beepers that might be on a corner?

**Answer:** This requires an unknown number of iterations of the **pickBeeper** instruction, so we can use the WHILE instruction to do this task too.

We can apply the four-step process for building WHILE loops and write the following implementation.

```
while ( nextToABeeper() )
{
        pickBeeper();
}
```

We simulate this and it appears to work. We now have to decide which loop to nest inside which loop. Do we put the loop that moves Karel to the southern boundary wall inside the loop that picks beepers or do we put the beeper-picking loop inside the loop that moves Karel to the wall?

**Question:** Can we interchange these two actions?

**Answer:** No, we cannot. Arriving at the wall should stop both Karel's moving and picking. Running out of beepers on one corner should **not** stop Karel's moving to the wall. As we move to the wall we can clean each corner of beepers if we nest the beeper-picking loop inside the loop that moves Karel to the wall.

Our new instruction definition will look like this:

```
void Beeper_Controller :: clearAllBeepersToTheWall()
{
      while ( frontIsClear() )
      {
            while ( nextToABeeper() )
            {
                  pickBeeper();
            }
            move();
      }
}
```

To solve the problem of deciding which WHILE loop is to be the outer loop, we can apply the <u>each test</u>. Do we need to pick up all of the beepers for **each** single step we take to the wall, or do we need to walk all the way to the wall for **each** single beeper that we pick up? Here, the answer is the former, and the outer loop is the stepping (move) loop.

When we nest WHILE loops we must be very sure that the execution of the nested loop (or inner loop) does not interfere with the test condition of the outer loop. In this problem the inner loop is responsible for picking beepers. The outer loop is responsible for moving the robot. These two activities do not affect each other, so the nesting seems correct.

We are not done; we must now test this new instruction. Trace Karel's execution of it using the initial situation shown in Figure 5-7. As much as we would like to believe it is correct, it isn't. We appear to have forgotten the fence post discussion of Section 5.3.1. The way we have written the new instruction, the last corner will not be cleared of beepers; this last corner is our forgotten fence post. To ensure that the last corner is cleared of beepers, we must make one more modification.

```
void Beeper_Controller :: clearAllBeepersToTheWall()
{
      while ( frontIsClear() )
      {
            while ( nextToABeeper() )
            {
                  pickBeeper();
            }
            move();
      }
      while ( nextToABeeper() )
      {
            pickBeeper();
      }
}
```

This third loop is outside the nested loops, and it will clear the last corner of beepers.

One note here about overall design of our new instruction: As a rule we prefer to perform only one task (such as moving to a wall) in a new instruction and move secondary tasks (such as picking the beepers) into a different new instruction. We believe that the following represents a better programming style for the previous new instruction.

```
void Beeper_Controller :: clearBeepersThisCorner()
{
      while ( nextToABeeper() )
      {
            pickBeeper();
      }
}

void Beeper_Controller :: clearAllBeepersToTheWall()
{
      while ( frontIsClear() )
      {
            clearBeepersThisCorner();
            move();
      }
      clearBeepersThisCorner();
}
```

This programming style is easier to read and, if we suddenly find that clearing the beepers requires a different strategy, we have only to make a change in one place, **clearBeepersThisCorner**.

### 5.4.2   A Bad Example of Nesting

A robot named Karel is facing south in the northwest corner of a room that has no doors or windows. Somewhere in the room, next to a wall, is a single beeper. Instruct Karel to find the beeper by writing the new instruction **findBeeper**. (See Figure 5-8).

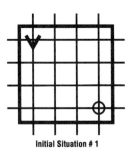

**Initial Situation # 1**

**Figure  5-8**   Initial Situation

We begin with our usual question-and-answer planning.

**Question:**  What is the problem?

**Answer:**   We must instruct Karel to find a beeper that is somewhere in the room next to the wall. We do not know how far away it is, and we do not know how big the room is.

**Question:**  What instruction can we use to move Karel to the beeper?

**Answer:**   Since the distance Karel must travel is unknown, we can use a WHILE loop.

Using the four-step process to build a WHILE loop, we develop the following new instruction:

```
void Beeper_Controller :: findBeeper()
{
     while ( ! nextToABeeper() )
     {
          move();
     }
}
```

If we carefully analyze this new instruction, we find, as shown in Figure 5-9, that Karel executes an error shutoff when it arrives at the southern wall.

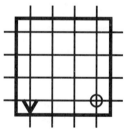

**Figure  5-9**  Karel Executes an Error Shutoff

**Question:**  What happened?

**Answer:**   We forgot about turning Karel at the corners.

**Question:**  How can we fix this problem?

**Answer:**   Let's walk Karel forward until it detects a wall.

**Question:**  What instruction can we use to do this?

**Answer:**   Since the distance Karel must travel is unknown, we can use a WHILE loop.

Again we use the four-step process to build a nested WHILE loop and develop the following new instruction:

```
void Beeper_Controller :: findBeeper()
{
      while ( ! nextToABeeper() )
      {
            while ( frontIsClear() )
            {
                  move();
            }
            turnLeft();
      }
}
```

We must test this to see whether it works. Because this problem is somewhat involved, we should use several different initial situations. Will the situations shown in Figure 5-10 be sufficient to test our code completely?

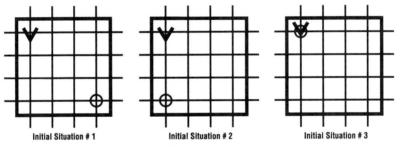

Initial Situation # 1          Initial Situation # 2          Initial Situation # 3

**Figure 5-10**   Three Different Initial Situations

If we trace our program using these situations, it appears that our instruction is correct. However, does the original problem statement guarantee that the beeper will always be in a corner? It does not. The original problem statement says that the beeper is somewhere next to a wall. Our three test situations each put the beeper in a corner. We should try an initial situation such as the one shown in Figure 5-11.

Let's see what happens here: Karel makes the outer test, `!nextToABeeper`, and it is true, so it begins to execute the outer loop body.

Karel makes the inner test, `frontIsClear`, which is true, so Karel moves forward one block, coming to rest on the corner with the beeper. What happens now? Karel remains focused on the inner loop. It has not forgotten about the outer loop, but its focus is restricted to the inner loop until the inner loop stops execution. Karel is required to make the inner test, `frontIsClear`, which is true, and moves one block forward, away from the beeper. Karel's situation is now as shown in Figure 5-12.

Karel remains focused on the inner loop and makes the inner test again. It is true, so Karel executes the move and is now in the situation shown in Figure 5-13.

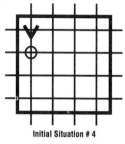

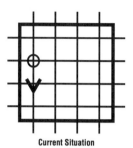

**Initial Situation # 4**

**Figure 5-11** Another Situation With Which to Test Our Instruction Definition

**Current Situation**

**Figure 5-12** Karel Misses the Beeper

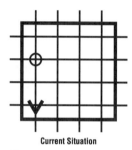

**Current Situation**

**Figure   5-13** Karel Arrives at the Wall

The inner test is false, so Karel ceases execution of the inner loop, executes the `turnLeft`, and is done with the first iteration of the outer loop. Now Karel makes the outer test, `!nextToABeeper`, which is true. Karel has no memory of once standing next to a beeper; consequently, Karel will continue to walk around this room and keep going and going and going. Our instruction will execute infinitely in this case.

There must be something wrong with our initial reasoning. Let's look at the initial planning segment.

**Question:**  What is the problem?

**Answer:**  We must instruct Karel to find a beeper that is somewhere in the room next to a wall. We do not know how far away it is, and we do not know how big the room is.

**Question:**  What instruction can we use to move Karel to the beeper?

**Answer:**  Since the distance Karel must travel is unknown, we can use a WHILE loop.

We then found that Karel performed an error shutoff because we instructed Karel to move forward when the front was blocked by a wall. Our next planning segment is as follows:

**Question:** What happened?

**Answer:** We forgot about turning Karel at the corners.

**Question:** How can we fix this problem?

**Answer:** Let's walk Karel forward until it detects a wall.

**Question:** What instruction can we use to do this?

**Answer:** Since the distance Karel must travel is unknown, we can use a WHILE loop.

This is where our plan began to go wrong. We decided to walk Karel forward until the front was blocked. We reasoned that we could use a WHILE loop to move Karel forward, and that was the mistake. If the robot moves more than one block forward without allowing the test of the outer WHILE loop to be checked, it will violate step 3 of the four-step process: "Do whatever is needed to ensure that the loop stops." Karel should move only one block forward within the outer WHILE loop. We should not use an inner WHILE loop to move Karel toward the wall. The reason is that Karel's execution of the inner WHILE loop can cause the outer WHILE loop to never stop. Both the outer and inner WHILE loops require Karel to execute the **move** instruction so that both loops will eventually terminate. Unless both tests, ! **nextToABeeper** and **frontIsClear**, are false at exactly the same time, the outer loop will never stop. We must discard the inner WHILE loop and find a different way to keep Karel from trying to move through the wall.

**Question:** How can we move Karel forward without the WHILE loop?

**Answer:** Karel should only move forward one block inside the WHILE loop so we must use an IF/ELSE statement to check for a wall. Karel will move when the front is clear and turn left when a wall is present.

Following our new reasoning, we have the following new instruction:

```
void Beeper_Controller :: findBeeper()
{
    while ( ! nextToABeeper() )
    {
        if ( frontIsClear() )
        {
            move();
        }
        else
        {
            turnLeft();
        }
    }
}
```

Nesting WHILE loops is a powerful programming idea, but with this increased power comes the increased need for very careful planning and analysis.

An alternative way to solve this is to start as previously with a simple WHILE loop, but suppose the existence of an instruction **moveTowardBeeper**.

```
void Beeper_Controller :: findBeeper()
{
      while ( ! nextToABeeper() )
      {
            moveTowardBeeper();
      }
}
```

What do we have to do to move toward the beeper? If we don't interpret it literally, but rather as "make one step of progress toward the goal of finding the beeper," then we easily arrive at the following:

```
void Beeper_Controller :: moveTowardBeeper()
{
      if ( frontIsClear() )
      {
            move();
      }
      else
      {
            turnLeft();
      }
}
```

## 5.5 WHILE AND IF INSTRUCTIONS

Novice programmers frequently use WHILE and IF instructions in a conflicting, unnecessary, or redundant manner. Examine the following program fragments to find improperly used tests.

```
if ( facingSouth() )
{
      while ( ! facingSouth() )
      {
            turnLeft();
      }
}
```

In this fragment there are conflicting tests. When the IF's test is true the WHILE's test must be false. This fragment will do nothing.

Let's try another one:

```
while ( ! frontIsClear())
{
        if ( frontIsClear())
        {
            move();
        }
        else
        {
            turnLeft();
        }
}
```

In this fragment there is an unnecessary test. When the WHILE's test is true, the IF's test must be false, so the ELSE is the only part of the loop body that is ever executed.

Here is another:

```
while ( nextToABeeper() )
{
        if ( nextToABeeper() )
        {
            pickBeeper();
        }
}
```

In this fragment there are redundant tests. The WHILE's test is the same as the IF's test. When the WHILE's test is true, so is the IF's.

Problems such as these usually enter our programs when we attempt to fix execution or intent errors. We sometimes get so involved in the details of our program that we forget to take a step back and look at the overall picture. It is often very helpful to take a break and come back to the program with fresh eyes.

## 5.6 REASONING ABOUT LOOPS

In Section 5.2.3 we discussed the four-step process for building a WHILE loop.

1. Identify the one test that must be true when the robot is finished with the loop.
2. Use the opposite form of the test identified in step 1 as the loop <test>.
3. Do what is needed to make progress toward solving the problem at hand and also ensure that the test eventually evaluates to false so that the WHILE loop stops.
4. Do whatever is required before or after the WHILE is executed to ensure that we solve the given problem.

We also presented an informal way to reason about the correctness of WHILE loops.

1.   Show that the instruction works correctly when the initial situation results in the test being false.

2.   Show that each time the loop body is executed, the robot's new situation is a simpler and similar version of the old situation.

We'd like to spend a little more time discussing this last concept of correctness. Remember that a robot will do exactly what it is told and only what it is told. It is up to us to make sure that it is provided with a correct way to solve a given problem. At the same time, we need a way to "prove" (in some sense) that our solution is correct. It will be impossible for us to simulate every possible situation, so we need a way to think through our solution in a formal way to verify that it does what it is supposed to do.

In order to reason about WHILE loops, we will need to understand a key concept called a <u>loop invariant</u>. A loop invariant is an assertion (something that can be proven true or false) that is true after each iteration of the loop. For our purposes, loop invariants will be assertions about the robot's world. In particular, the items that we need to be concerned about after one iteration are the following:

-   How has the robot's direction changed, if at all?
-   How has the robot's relative position in the world changed, if at all (this may involve thinking about wall segments as well)?
-   How has the number of beepers in the robot's beeper-bag changed, if at all?
-   How have the number and location of other beepers in the world changed, if at all?

Let's look at these items using the example given in Section 5.2.4, the instruction `clearAllBeepersToTheWall`. After one iteration of the following loop,

```
while ( frontIsClear() )
{
    move();
    pickBeeper();
}
```

what can we say (assert) about the items just mentioned? We can assert the following:

-   The robot's direction is unchanged.
-   The robot's position has been advanced one corner.
-   That corner has one less beeper.
-   The robot's beeper-bag has another beeper.

Which of these statements are "interesting"? By *interesting* we mean which item is important in terms of the problem being solved. Since we are removing beepers from the world as the robot moves forward, we are interested in the second and third assertions. A loop invariant captures the interesting change during one iteration of the loop. Thus, for this problem, the loop invariant is that the robot has advanced one corner and removed one beeper from that corner.

What else have we learned? Let's look at our loop test, `frontIsClear`. When the loop ends, it will be false, and thus the front will be blocked. So we know that when the loop terminates, the robot has removed one beeper from each corner it has passed and the robot's front is now blocked. We have learned that as long as each corner had one beeper on it, our loop must have solved the problem of picking up beepers to the wall.

Let's look at the fence post problem presented in Section 5.3.1. What is the loop invariant for the first attempt at solving that problem? Here's the loop:

```
while ( frontIsClear() )
{
        pickBeeper();
        move();
}
```

What can we assert about this loop?

- The robot's direction is unchanged.
- The robot's position has been advanced forward one corner.
- The previous corner has one less beeper.
- The robot's beeper-bag has one more beeper.

What do we know about the robot and the world when the loop finishes? We know that any previous corners have had one beeper removed from them. Finally, we know that the robot's front is blocked.

What about the robot's current corner? Since the loop invariant mentions only previous corners, we know nothing about the corner on which the robot is standing when the loop terminates—it may have a beeper, it may not. How we choose to remedy this situation is up to us, but at least in reasoning about the loop we have become aware of a potential problem with our loop: the fence post problem.

Loop invariants can be powerful tools in aiding our understanding of how a loop is operating and what it will cause a robot to do. The key lies in determining how executing the loop changes the state of the world during each iteration and capturing that change as succinctly as possible. Once we've discovered the loop invariant, we can use it and the loop's termination condition to decide whether the loop solves the problem. If not, we must look back over the steps for constructing a WHILE loop to see where we might have gone wrong.

Another use of loop invariants is to help us determine what instructions we want to use in the loop body. So far we've used the loop invariant as an after-the-fact device, to verify that a loop we've written solves a specific problem. If we decide what we want the invariant to be before we write the body of the loop, it can help in deciding what the body should be. As an example, consider the following problem: A robot is searching for a beeper that is an unknown distance directly in front of it and there may be some one-block-high wall segments in the way.

What do we want to be true when the loop terminates? Since the robot is looking for a beeper, we want it to be next to a beeper. Thus our test is ! nextToABeeper. What do we want to be invariant? The robot must move one (and only one) block forward during each iteration of the loop to ensure that each corner is examined. Our first pass at a loop might look like this:

```
while ( ! nextToABeeper() )
{
        move();
}
```

Unfortunately, this will cause an error shutoff if we happen to run into one of those intervening wall segments before reaching the beeper. How can we maintain our invariant and still avoid the wall segment? A little insight might suggest the following modification:

```
while ( ! nextToABeeper() )
{
        if ( frontIsClear() )
        {
                move();
        }
        else
        {
                avoidWall();
        }
}
```

where avoidWall is defined as follows:

```
void Beeper_Controller :: avoidWall()
{
        turnLeft();
        move();
        turnRight();
        move();
        turnRight();
        move();
        turnLeft();
}
```

In defining avoidWall, we must keep the loop invariant in mind. We want to make progress toward our goal, but as little progress as possible so that we don't accidentally miss something. We should spend some time convincing ourselves that this loop does indeed maintain the initial invariant: that the robot moves one (and only one) block forward during each iteration of the loop. If we can do this we can also convince ourselves that this loop does solve the problem.

## 5.7 A LARGE PROGRAM WRITTEN BY STEPWISE REFINEMENT

In this section we will write a complex program by using stepwise refinement. Suppose that we need to patrol the perimeter of a rectangular field of beepers. Imagine that there has been theft of the beepers and we need a robot guard to walk around the edge of the field. Let us build a class of **Guard** robots with an instruction **walkPerimeter**. The robot will initially be positioned somewhere in the field, perhaps but not necessarily on an edge.

To make the problem more definite, let's suppose that the field is at least two beepers wide and two beepers long. The path we want the robot to follow is one that walks along corners that actually contain the beepers marking the outer edge of the field. In the sample initial situation shown in Figure 5-14, the path should include 2nd and 9th Streets and 3rd and 7th Avenues.

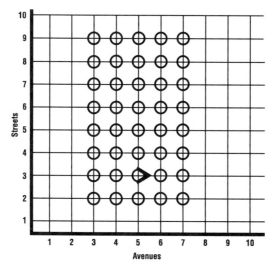

**Figure 5-14** Initial Situation

As an initial strategy suppose that we walk our robot, say Tony, to the southeast corner and have it walk the perimeter from there. We may need other instructions to help us build these, but a first approximation to our class definition is as follows:

```
class Guard: Robot
}
```

```
void moveToSouthEastCorner();
void walkPerimeter();
    . . .
};
```

First let's attack the **walkPerimeter** instruction, assuming that we can begin it at the southeast corner. Since it is easier for a robot to turn left (faster anyway) than to turn right, let's program the robot to walk around the field in a counterclockwise direction, turning left at each corner. Since there are four edges to be walked, we can use a loop instruction. For each execution of the body of the loop we should walk one edge and then turn left at the end of it.

```
void Guard::walkPerimeter() // Robot begins at a
                            // corner of the field
{
      loop(4)
      {
            followEdge();
            turnLeft();
      }
}
```

This solution, of course, requires us to add an additional instruction, **followEdge**, to the **Guard** class. What does it take to follow an edge? Since the edge is marked by beepers, the robot can simply move along it until there is no beeper on the current corner.

```
void Guard::followEdge() // Robot starts on a
                         // corner with a beeper
{
      while (nextToABeeper())
      {
            move();
      }
}
```

If we try to simulate this by hand, we find an error. After executing **followEdge**, Tony is left on a corner without any beepers. Since **turnLeft** doesn't change the corner, we find that after executing **followEdge** and then **turnLeft** once, we are not in a legal position to execute **followEdge** again. What actually happens when we execute **followEdge** is that Tony walks outside the field and then turns completely around in place. Suppose that we have Tony back up as the last step in **followEdge**, so that it is left on a corner with a beeper. Backing up requires that the robot be able to turn around. Thus we must add the following:

```
void Guard::turnAround()
{
        turnLeft();
        turnLeft();
}

void Guard::backUp()
{
        turnAround();
        move();
        turnAround();
}
```

Now we can correct `followEdge`:

```
void Guard::followEdge()  // Robot starts on a
                          // corner with a beeper
{
        while (nextToABeeper())
        {
                move();
        }
        backUp();
}
```

Now our simulation seems correct, so we turn to **moveToSouthEastCorner**. To do this we can have the robot face south and then move until it is on the edge of the field, turn left, and then walk until it reaches the corner. Facing south is not especially difficult because we have a test for facing south.

```
void Guard:: faceSouth()
{
        while (! facingSouth())
        {
                turnLeft();
        }
}
```

To move to the south edge of the field, Tony now just needs to walk until there is no beeper on the current corner and then back up. But that is exactly what **followEdge** does.

```
void Guard:: moveToSouthEastCorner()
{
        faceSouth();
        followEdge();
```

```
        // Now at south edge of field
    turnLeft();
    followEdge();
        // Now at southeast corner of field
}
```

We have carried out our plan, but when we execute it we find that the robot walks around only three sides of the field, not all four, although it does walk part of the fourth side while it is moving to the southeast corner. What is wrong? The individual instructions seem to do what they were designed to do, but they don't fit together very well. The problem is that after executing **moveToSouthEastCorner**, the robot is left facing east. Then, when we ask it to **walkPerimeter** it begins by walking immediately outside the field. The first execution of **followEdge** has taken us outside the field and then back to the corner, "wasting" one of our four executions of **followEdge**. We should make the <u>postconditions</u> of one instruction match up better with the <u>preconditions</u> of the next. A precondition for an instruction is a predicate that the caller of an instruction is required to establish before executing the instruction to guarantee its correct behavior. For example, a precondition for the **pickBeeper** instruction is that the robot be on a corner with a beeper. A postcondition for an instruction is the predicate that is guaranteed to be true when an instruction completes, if all of its preconditions were true before it was executed. The postcondition of the **pickBeeper** instruction is that the robot has at least one beeper in its beeper-bag.

Suppose that we add an additional postcondition to **moveToSouthEastCorner** and require that it turn at the end of its walk to put the field to the left of the robot. We can achieve this by adding a **turnLeft** to the end of **moveToSouthEastCorner**.

```
    void Guard:: moveToSouthEastCorner()
    {
        faceSouth();
        followEdge();
        // Now at south edge of field
        turnLeft();
        followEdge();
        turnLeft();
        // Now at southeast corner of field
        // facing north
    }
```

Putting all of this together, we get the **Guard** class:

```
    class Guard: Robot
    }
        void moveToSouthEastCorner();
        void walkPerimeter();
        void backUp();
```

```
        void faceSouth();
        void turnAround();
        void followEdge();
};
```

Now, when we simulate our robot, it will correctly follow all four edges of the field of Figure 5-14. When we try it in other legal fields, however, we find that we have trouble. For example, we find that Tony will execute an error shutoff in trying to patrol the field Of Figure 5-15.

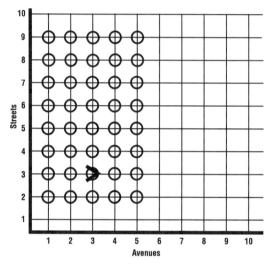

**Figure 5-15**    Another Initial Position

We call this type of situation a <u>beyond-the-horizon situation</u>. Normally, we write a program guided by a few initial situations that seem to cover all interesting aspects of the task. Although we would like to prove that all other situations are not too different from these sample situations, frequently the best we can do is hope. As we explore the problem and learn more about the task, we may discover situations that are beyond our original horizons, situations that are legal but special trouble-causing cases. Once we suspect a beyond-the-horizon situation, we should immediately simulate a robot's execution in it. If our suspicions are confirmed, and the robot does not perform as we intended, we must modify our program accordingly.

We must reprogram the robot to realize that it is at the edge of a field as soon as it contacts a wall, as well as when it is no longer at a beeper. Because all of our edge sensing is in `followEdge`, we look there for a solution.

Here is a solution in which we need stop moving when either `!nextToABeeper` or `!frontIsClear` becomes true. Therefore the opposite of this is our condition for continuing to move. We want to say

```
    while (nextToABeeper() AND frontIsClear()) . . .
```

This is a natural place for a new predicate. It is quite simple:

```
Boolean Guard::nextToABeeper_and_frontIsClear()
{       if( nextToABeeper() )
        {
                return frontIsClear();
        }
        return false;
}
```

It will be instructive to try to use nested constructs as in Chapter 4. Here, however, we have WHILE instructions and not IF instructions. Often the correct solution to this is to nest an IF instruction inside of a WHILE instruction. Suppose we try each of the following to see if they might help us here.

```
while(nextToABeeper())              while(frontIsClear())
{                                   {
        if(frontIsClear())                 if(nextToABeeper())
        {                                  {
                move();                            move();
        }                                  }
}                                   }
```

The second one seems clearly wrong; once a robot begins executing, execution will continue until it encounters a wall. Because walls aren't necessarily part of the problem, the robot will walk too far afield.

The first seems to be fine until we simulate it in our beyond-the-horizon situation, in which it will continue to execute forever. The problem is that when we encounter the wall, we are still on a corner with a beeper, and so we don't exit from the WHILE. We can solve this, however, by picking up the beeper in this situation.

```
while(nextToABeeper())
{
        if(frontIsClear())
        {
                move();
        }
        else
        {
                pickBeeper();
        }
}
```

Now we will exit, but we must replace the beeper that we may have picked up. After we exit this WHILE loop, we know that there is no beeper on the current corner, but we don't know whether we picked one up or not. We could simply ask the robot to put a beeper if it has any, but this requires that the robot begin with no beepers in its beeper-bag. What else do we know? Well, we know that if we picked up a beeper it was because our front was blocked and we haven't moved or turned, so its front must still be blocked in that case. If it is not blocked, it is because we have walked off the edge of the field to an empty corner.

```
void Guard::followEdge() // Robot starts on a corner
                         // with a beeper
{
    while(nextToABeeper())
    {
        if(frontIsClear())
        {
            move();
        }
        else
        {
            pickBeeper();
        }
    }
    if(frontIsBlocked())
    {
        putBeeper();
    }
    else
    {
        backUp();
    }
}
```

As it often happens in programming, just when we think we have a solution to a programming problem, the problem changes. When the owner of the field saw our solution in action, she observed that the robot wasn't going to be especially effective in preventing beeper theft because, while Tony was walking along one edge, some-one could steal beepers by entering from the opposite edge. To prevent this, she has changed the specification of the problem to require four robots, starting the four corners of the field, all walking in unison, to keep better watch. We will look at this problem in the exercises of Chapter 6.

## 5.8  WHEN TO USE A REPEATING INSTRUCTION

As explained at the end of the last chapter, a decision map is a technique that asks questions about the problem we are trying to solve. The answers to the questions determine which path of the map to follow. If we have done a thorough job of planning our implementation, the decision map should suggest an appropriate instruction to use.

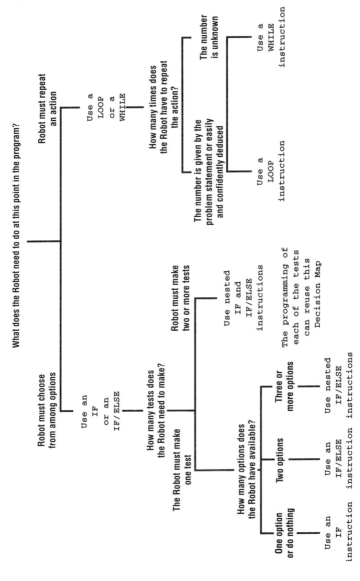

**Figure 5-16**   A Complete Decision Map

Take some time and examine some of the discussions presented in this chapter and see how the complete decision map, which is presented in Figure 5-16, might have been useful.

## 5.9  PROBLEM SET

The problems in this section require writing definitions and programs that use LOOP and WHILE instructions. Try using stepwise refinement and the four-step process discussed in Section 5.2.3 when writing these definitions and programs. Test your solutions by simulating them in various initial situations, and try to find beyond-the-horizon situations, too. Take care to write programs that avoid error shutoffs and infinite loops.

A common mistake among beginning programmers is trying to have each execution of a WHILE loop's body make too much progress. As a rule of thumb, try to have each execution of a WHILE loop's body make as little progress as possible (while still making some progress toward terminating the loop).

1.  Write a new instruction named **emptyBeeperBag**. After a robot executes this instruction, its beeper-bag should be empty.

2.  Write a new instruction called **goToOrigin** that positions a robot on 1st Street and 1st Avenue facing east, regardless of its initial location or the direction it is initially facing. Assume that there are no wall sections present. *Hint:* Use the south and west boundary walls as guides.

3.  Study both of the following program fragments separately. What does each do? For each, is there a simpler program fragment that is execution equivalent? If so, write it down; if not, explain why not.

```
while( ! nextToABeeper())        while( ! nextToABeeper())
{                                {
      move();                        if(nextToABeeper())
}                                    {
if(nextToABeeper())                      pickBeeper();
{                                    }
      pickBeeper();                  else
}                                    {
else                                     move();
{                                    }
      move();                    }
}
```

Describe the difference between the following two program fragments:

```
while(frontIsClear())            if(frontIsClear())
    {                                {
```

```
        move();                              move();
}                                    }
```

4.  There is a menace in Karel's world: an infinite pile of beepers. Yes, it sounds impossible, but occasionally one occurs in the world. If Karel accidentally tries to pick up an infinite pile of beepers, it is forever doomed to pick up beepers from the pile. Karel's current situation places the robot in grave danger from such a pile. The robot is standing outside two rooms: one is to the west and one is to the east. Only one of these rooms has a pile of beepers that Karel can pick. The other room has the dreaded infinite pile of beepers. Karel must decide which room is the safe room, enter it, and pick up all of the beepers. To help the robot decide which room is safe, there is a third pile of beepers on the corner at which Karel is currently standing. If this third pile has an even number of beepers, the safe room is the eastern room. If the pile has an odd number of beepers, the safe room is the western room. There is at least one beeper in the third pile. Program Karel to pick the beepers in the safe room (see Figure 5-17).

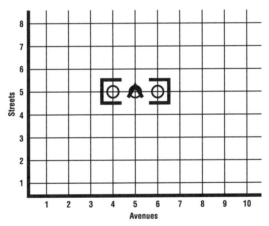

**Figure 5-17**  A Very Dangerous Task

5.  A robot must place beepers in the exact arrangement shown in Figure 5-18. Assume that it starts with exactly enough beepers for the task and always starts on the bottom-left corner of the square.

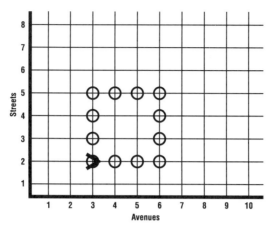

**Figure 5-18**    A Beeper-Arranging Task

6. Instruct a robot to escape from any rectangular room that has an open doorway exactly one block wide. After the robot has escaped from the room, the program must command the robot to turn itself off.

7. Program a robot to escape from a rectangular room if it can find a doorway. If there is no doorway, the robot must turn itself off. We may not be able to use the program written in Problem 6 for this task, because executing this program in a doorless room could cause the robot to run around inside the room forever. *Hint:* There is a slightly messy way to solve this problem without resorting to beepers. You can write the program this way, or you can assume that the robot has one beeper in the beeper-bag, which it can use to remember if it has circumnavigated the room. This program may require a separate **turnOff** instruction for the completely enclosed situation in addition to a **turnOff** instruction for the situation with a door.

8. Karel is working once again as a gardener. Karel must outline the wall segment shown in Figure 5-19 with beepers. One and only one beeper is to be planted on each corner that is adjacent to a wall. You may assume that Karel always starts in the same relative position and has exactly enough beepers to do the task.

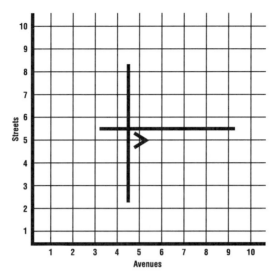

**Figure 5-19**  Another Gardening Job

9. Karel's beeper crop failed again. The robot is back to carpeting hallways. The hallways always have the same general shape as shown in Figure 5-20 and are always one block wide. To ensure there are no lumps in the carpet, only one beeper can be placed on a corner. Karel has exactly enough beepers to do the job and always starts in the same relative location.

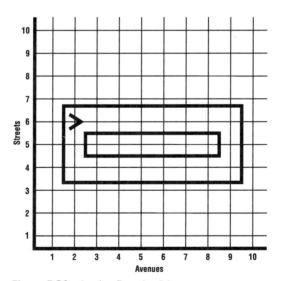

**Figure 5-20**  Another Carpeting Job

10. Program a robot to run a super steeplechase. In this race the hurdles are arbitrarily high and the course has no fixed finish corner. The finish of each race course is marked by a beeper that the robot must pick up before turning itself

off. Figure 5-21 illustrates one possible course. Other courses may be longer and have higher hurdles. Should you modify the class you built in Problem 6 of Chapter 4 or build a new class?

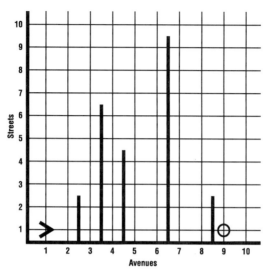

**Figure 5-21**   A Super Steeplechase

11. Program a robot to run a super-duper steeplechase. In this race the hurdles are arbitrarily high and arbitrarily wide. In each race course the finish is marked by a beeper, which the robot must pick up before turning itself off. Figure 5-22 illustrates one possible race course. The best way to do this exercise, of course, is to build a subclass of the **Steeplechaser** class you built in Problem 10.

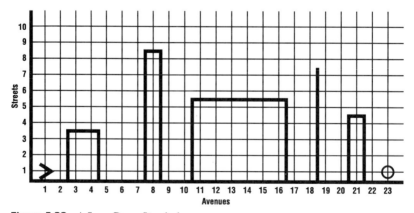

**Figure 5-22**   A Super-Duper Steeplechase

12. Write an instruction that harvests a rectangular field of any size. The field is guaranteed to be bordered by beeperless corners. Also assume that every corner within the field has a beeper on it and that our robot starts facing east on the lower left-hand corner of the field. Should we use a class derived from **Harvester**?

13. Karel has returned to the diamond-shaped beeper field (see Figure 5-23) to harvest a new crop. Write a new program for Karel that harvests the beepers. The beeper field is always the same size, and there is always one beeper on each corner of the field.

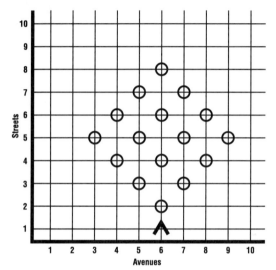

**Figure 5-23**   Return to the Diamond-Shaped Beeper Field

14. A robot named Karel is building a fence. The fence will be made of beepers and will surround a rectangular-shaped wall segment. The size of the wall segment is unknown. Karel is at the origin facing an unknown direction. The fences (beepers) are stacked somewhere next to the western boundary wall. There are exactly enough beepers in the pile to build the fence. The beeper pile is on the street that is adjacent to the southern edge of the wall segment, as shown in the Figure 5-24. The distances to the beeper pile and to the wall segment are unknown. Program Karel to build the fence and return to the origin. Assume that there are no beepers in Karel's beeper-bag at the start of the program.

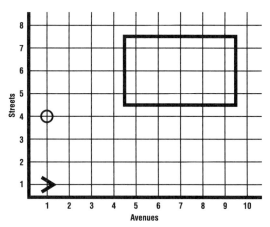

**Figure 5-24** Building a Fence

15. A robot named Karel likes to take long, meandering walks in the woods in the world, and even though it has a built-in compass, the robot sometimes cannot find its way back home. To alleviate this problem, before Karel walks in the woods the robot fills its beeper-bag and then it leaves a trail of beepers. Program Karel to follow this path back home. There are many questions one can ask about this task. Ignore the possibility that any wall boundaries or wall sections interfere with Karel, and assume that the end of the path is marked by two beepers on the same corner. Each beeper will be reachable from the previous beeper by the execution of one move. Also, the path will never cross over itself. See Figure 5-25 for a path that Karel must follow. *Hint:* Karel must probe each possible next corner in the path, eventually finding the correct one. It might prove useful to have Karel pick up the beepers as it follows the path; otherwise it may get caught in an infinite loop going backward and forward. How difficult would it be to program Karel to follow the same type of path if we allowed for a beeper to be missing occasionally (but not two missing beepers in a row)?

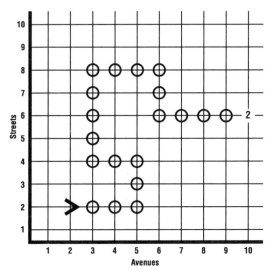

**Figure 5-25** A Path of Beepers

16. Assume that a robot is somewhere in a completely enclosed rectangular room that contains one beeper. Program the robot to find the beeper, pick it up, and turn itself off.

17. Program a robot named Karel to escape from a maze that contains no islands. The exit of the maze is marked by placing a beeper on the first corner that is outside the maze, next to the right wall. This task can be accomplished by commanding Karel to move through the maze, with the invariant that its right side is always next to a wall. See Problem 9 in Section 4.10 for hints on the type of movements for which Karel must be programmed. Figure 5-26 shows one example of a maze.

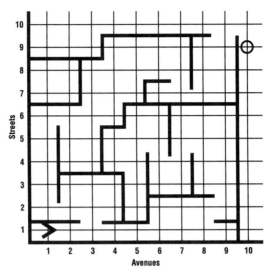

**Figure 5-26** A Maze

There is a simpler way to program this task without using the instructions written in Problem 9 in Section 4.9. Try to write a shorter version of the maze-escaping program. *Hint:* Program Karel to make the least amount of progress toward its goal at each corner in the maze.

Finally, compare the maze escape problem with Problem 10 in Section 5.9, the super-duper steeplechase. Do you see any similarities? Are there any similarities to the room-escaping problem? What class should we build to solve this problem? What should the parent class be?

18. This problem is inspired by the discussion on the verification of WHILE loops (Section 5.6). Simulate a robot's execution of the following instruction in initial situations where the robot is on a corner with zero, one, two, three, and seven beepers.

```
void Beeper_Controller :: willThisClearCornerOfBeepers()
{
    loop (10)
    {
        if ( nextToABeeper() )
        {
            pickBeeper();
        }
    }
}
```

State in exactly which initial situations this instruction works correctly. What happens in the other situations?

**19.** Program a robot named Karel to go on a treasure hunt. The treasure is marked by a corner containing five beepers. Other corners (including the corner on which Karel starts) contain clues, with each clue indicating in which direction Karel should proceed. The clues are as follows: one beeper means that Karel should go north, two means west, three means south, and four means east. Karel should follow the clues until it reaches the treasure corner, where the robot should turn itself off. Figure 5-27 shows one possible treasure hunt.

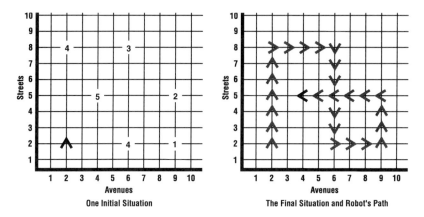

**One Initial Situation**    **The Final Situation and Robot's Path**

**Figure 5-27**    A Treasure Hunt

**20.** A robot named Karel is inside a room as shown in Figure 5-28 that has a number of open windows. There are no windows in the corners of the room. Karel is next to the northern wall facing east. Program Karel to close the windows by putting one beeper in front of each window. You may assume that Karel has exactly enough beepers to complete the task.

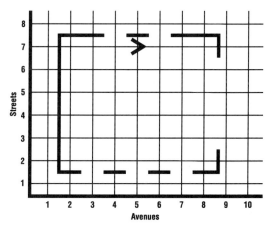

**Figure 5-28**    Closing the Windows

21.  A robot named Karel is at the origin facing east. In front of Karel, somewhere along 1st Street, is a line of beepers (one beeper is on each corner, with at least one beeper in the line). The length of the line of beepers is unknown, but there are no gaps in the line. Karel must pick up and move the beepers north a number of streets equal to the number of beepers in the line. For example, if there are five beepers in the line, the beepers must be moved to 6th Street. The beepers must be moved directly north. If the first beeper is on 4th Avenue, it must be on 4th Avenue when the program is finished.

22.  A robot named Karel is inside a completely enclosed room with no doors or windows, as shown in Figure 5-29. The robot is in the southeast corner facing south. There is one wall segment inside the room with Karel. The wall segment blocks north/south travel and does not touch the walls that form the room. On one side of the wall segment is a beeper (which side is unknown). Program Karel to find and move the beeper to the opposite side of the wall segment.

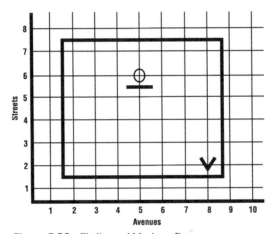

**Figure 5-29**  Finding and Moving a Beeper

23.  Once again Karel is working as a carpet layer. Before carpeting a room Karel must ensure that the room has continuous walls to the west, north, and east. Only these rooms must be carpeted. The doors to the rooms are always to the south. All rooms are one block wide, and there is always a northern wall at the end of each room. Karel's task ends when the robot arrives at a blocking wall segment on 1st Street. Figure 5-30 shows one possible set of initial and final situations.

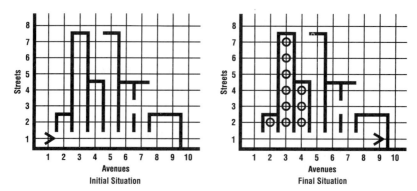

**Figure 5-30** A More Complex Carpet-Laying Task

24. What will be the effect of executing the following instruction?

```
while (facingNorth())
{
        turnLeft();
}
```

25. Program a robot named Karel to arrange vertical piles of beepers into ascending order. Each avenue, starting at the origin, will contain a vertical pile of one or more beepers. The first empty avenue will mark the end of the piles that need to be sorted. Figure 5-31 illustrates one of the many possible initial and final situations. (How difficult would it be to modify your program to arrange the piles of beepers into descending order?)

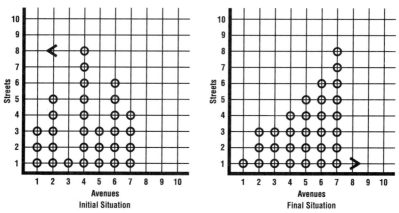

**Figure 5-31** A Sorting Task

26. Build a new robot **Sweeper** class, derived from the **Robot** class of Chapter 4. The defining property of robots in this class is that they sweep up all beep-

ers on any corner to which they move. Why is this not quite the same thing as saying that they sweep up all beepers on all corners that they occupy?

**27.** Program the three robots Karel, Carol, and Karl to run a relay super steeple-chase. Karel will start the race at the origin with one beeper in its beeper-bag. Somewhere along 1st Street Carol will be waiting. When Karel gets to Carol, Karel should pass the beeper to Carol, Carol should continue the race, and Karel should stop. When Carol gets to Karl, Karl should likewise continue, with the beeper, and stop only when it comes to a corner with a beeper marking the end of the course. It should put down the beeper it is carrying at this final corner. You may want to put Karel and Carol in a different class than Karl, who can be a Steeplechaser robot. Here you will get a chance to use the predicate **nextToARobot**.

**28.** Tony the robot is standing at the origin with some beepers in its beeper-bag. Write an instruction that will deposit half of the beepers on the corner. The others should be retained in the beeper-bag. If there are an odd number of beepers, then the extra one should be left on the corner.

# 6 ADVANCED TECHNIQUES FOR ROBOTS

This chapter presents a number of quite challenging topics. First we will introduce the concept of recursion. Recursion, like loops, allows robots to execute a sequence of statements more than once. We will also look at the formal relationship between recursion and loops. Next we study two interesting new instructions that give robots the ability to solve some novel beeper-manipulation problems, including numerical computations. Then we will look again at object-oriented programming and see some implications of what we have learned here.

## 6.1  INTRODUCTION TO RECURSION

Having thoroughly looked at loops in the last chapter, we are now going to examine a different way to get a robot to repeat an action. The technique is called <u>recursion</u>. The word means, simply, to recur or repeat. When a programming language allows <u>recursive definitions</u> or recursion, it means that a new instruction can call itself (use its own name) within its own definition. This may seem odd at first, but after a few examples, we hope that it will appear as natural as using a WHILE loop to control a robot's execution. We note that recursion is just another control structure and, while it may appear magical at first, it can be understood as readily as loops. It is another programming tool to add to your collection.

In all of the examples prior to Chapter 5, when we asked a robot to move from one point to another, we knew exactly how far it would move. There are many situations, however, in which this is not true. Suppose, for example, that a robot named Kristin is standing at the origin facing east, and suppose that there is a beeper somewhere along 1st Street. We want Kristin to go to the beeper and pick it up and return to the origin.

```
Kristin.retrieveBeeper ();
```

If we knew that the beeper was on 1st and 23rd, we would be able to write a program without loops to do this. If we knew that it was no more than, say, 15 blocks away, then we could find a solution. (How?) But what if we don't know how far it is? To get started, let's build a new class: `Beeper_Finder`.

```
class Beeper_Finder: Robot
{
        void retrieveBeeper ();
        void findBeeper();
        void returnToWestWall();
};

void Beeper_Finder :: retrieveBeeper ()
{
        findBeeper();
        pickBeeper();
        turnLeft();
        turnLeft();
        returnToWestWall();
}
```

That will certainly do the job, if we can write the other two new instructions. Let's now attack **findBeeper**. We know that there is a beeper somewhere on 1st Street. We also know that Kristin is on 1st Street facing east. It may be that Kristin is already on the beeper corner, in which case there is nothing to do. Therefore we may get started by writing

```
void Beeper_Finder :: findBeeper()
{
        if (! nextToABeeper())
        {
            ...
        }
}
```

This will correctly terminate having done nothing if Kristin is already at the beeper corner. Suppose next that the beeper is on some other corner. Then Kristin needs to move, of course, and check other corners.

```
void Beeper_Finder :: findBeeper()
{
        if (! nextToABeeper())
        {
            move();
            ???
        }
}
```

Well, what does Kristin need to do after a move? Notice that Kristin is on a different corner than the one on which it started and that the original corner was checked and found to lack a beeper. Therefore we may conclude that the beeper is now (after the move) either at Kristin's current location or farther east of it. But this is just the same situation (relatively) that Kristin was in when it started this task. Therefore we can conclude that what Kristin needs to do now is exactly **findBeeper** and nothing more.

```
void Beeper_Finder :: findBeeper()
{
        if (! nextToABeeper())
        {
            move();
            findBeeper();
        }
}
```

Notice that **findBeeper** has been completely defined, but it has been defined by using **findBeeper** itself. How can this be done? Well, suppose we needed to empty an ocean with a bucket. To perform **emptyTheOcean**, we first ask if the ocean is empty. If so, we are done. Otherwise we just remove one bucket of water from the ocean and then **emptyTheOcean**.

The important thing in such a definition, called a recursive definition, is that we don't define a thing in terms of precisely itself. We define a thing in terms of a simpler or smaller version of itself, and also define the smallest or simplest version separately. Here we define **findBeeper** as either "nothing", if Kristin is already on the beeper corner, or **move(); findBeeper();**, if Kristin is anywhere else. It is also necessary to know before we start executing such an instruction that there is indeed a beeper somewhere in Kristin's path. Otherwise, after every move, the reexecution of **findBeeper** will find that the test is true, generating yet another reexecution of **findBeeper** without end.

The other instruction, **returnToWestWall**, is similar, except for the test. Here, however we know that there is a wall to the west. If we can guarantee that the robot is also facing west, then the following instruction will serve:

```
void Beeper_Finder :: returnToWestWall()
{
        if (frontIsClear())
        {
            move();
            returnToWestWall();
        }
}
```

Programming with recursion is a very powerful and sometimes error-prone activity.

## 6.2 MORE ON RECURSION

Given the problem—a robot must clean all beepers from its current corner—we could easily write a loop that looks like the following:

```
void Sweeper :: sweepCorner()
{
        while ( nextToABeeper() )
        {
                pickBeeper();
        }
}
```

This correctly solves the problem and is known as an iterative solution (*iterative* means that a loop of some sort, WHILE or LOOP, was used). Contrast this solution with a recursive one:

```
void Sweeper :: sweepCorner()
{
        if ( nextToABeeper() )
        {
                pickBeeper();
                sweepCorner();
        }
}
```

The difference between these two instructions is very subtle. The first instruction, which uses the WHILE loop, is called once and the robot's focus never leaves the loop until it is finished, executing zero or more **pickBeepers** (depending on the initial number on the corner). What happens in the second, recursive, **sweepCorner**? Let's look at it very carefully.

If the robot is initially on an empty corner when the instruction is called, nothing happens (similar to the WHILE loop). If it is on a corner with one beeper when the instruction is called, the IF test is true, so the robot executes one **pickBeeper** instruction (thus emptying the corner). It then makes a second call of **sweepCorner**, remembering where it was in the first call. When **sweepCorner** is called the second time, the IF test is false, so nothing happens and the robot returns to the first call.

Initial instantiation:

```
void Sweeper :: sweepCorner()
{
        if ( nextToABeeper() )
        {
                pickBeeper();
```

```
                  sweepCorner();  // <-- This is the
                                  // second call to
         }                        // sweepCorner.
                                  // The robot will
                                  // return to this
}                                 // point when that
                                  // call finishes
                                  // executing.
```

Second instantiation:

```
void Sweeper :: sweepCorner()
{
         if ( nextToABeeper() )  // <-- this is now
                                 // false
         {
                  pickBeeper();
                  sweepCorner();
         }
}
```

Each of these calls results in a separate instance (or instantiation) of the instruction **sweepCorner**. The robot must completely execute each instance, always remembering where it was in the previous instance so it can return there when it finishes.

The process for writing recursive robot instructions is very similar to that for writing loops:

*Step 1.* Consider the stopping condition (also called the base case)—what is the simplest case of the problem that can be solved? In the **sweepCorner** problem, the simplest, or base, case is when the robot is already on an empty corner.

*Step 2.* What does the robot have to do in the base case? In this example there's nothing to do.

*Step 3.* Find a way to solve a small piece of the larger problem if not in the base case. This is called "reducing the problem in the general case." In the **sweepCorner** problem, the general case is when the robot is on a corner with one or more beepers and the reduction is to pick up a beeper.

*Step 4.* Make sure the reduction leads to the base case. Again, in the example of **sweepCorner**, by picking up one beeper at a time, the robot must eventually clear the corner of beepers regardless of the original number present.

Let's compare and contrast iteration and recursion:

• An iterative loop must complete each iteration before beginning the next one.

• A recursive instruction typically begins a new instance before completing the current one. When that happens, the current instance is temporarily suspended, pending the completion of the new instance. Of course, this new instance might not complete before generating another one. Each successive instance must be completed in turn, last to first.

- Since **each** recursive instance is supposed to make some (often minimal) progress toward the base case, we should not use loops to control recursive calls. Thus we will usually see an IF or an IF/ELSE in the body of a recursive new instruction, but not a WHILE.

Suppose we wanted to use recursion to move a robot named Karel to a beeper. How would we do it? Following the steps presented earlier,

- What is the base case? Karel is on the beeper.
- What does the robot have to do in the base case? Nothing.
- What is the general case? The robot is not on the beeper.
- What is the reduction? Move toward the beeper and make the recursive call.
- Does the reduction lead to termination? Yes, assuming the beeper is directly in front of the robot , the distance will be shortened by one block for each recursive call.

The final implementation follows:

```
void Beeper_Controller :: findBeeper()
{
        if ( ! nextToABeeper() )
        {
            move();
            findBeeper();
        }
}
```

Note that this problem could also have been easily solved with a WHILE loop. Let's look at a problem that is not easily solved with a WHILE loop. Remember the Lost Beeper Mine, the corner with a large number of beepers? Imagine we must write the following instruction in our search for the mine. A robot named Karel must walk east from its current location until it finds a beeper. The Lost Beeper Mine is due north of that intersection a distance equal to the number of moves Karel made to get from its current position to the beeper. Write the new instruction **findMine**.

It is not easy to see how to solve this problem with a WHILE loop because we do not have any convenient way of remembering how many intersections have been traversed. We could probably come up with a very convoluted beeper-tracking scheme, but let's look at a recursive solution that's pretty straightforward. Again, we'll answer our questions:

- What is the base case? Karel is on the beeper.
- What does Karel have to do in the base case? **turnLeft** (this will face Karel north).

- What is the general case? Karel is not on the beeper.
- What is the reduction? Move one block forward, make the recursive call and have Karel execute a second move after the recursive call. This second move will be executed in all instances but the base case, causing Karel to make as many moves north after the base case as it did in getting to the base case.
- Does the reduction lead to termination? Yes, assuming the beeper is directly in front of Karel.

Let's look at the complete instruction:

```
void Prospector :: findMine()
{
        if ( nextToABeeper() )
        {
             turnLeft();
        }
        else
        {
             move();
             findMine();
             move();
        }
}
```

How many **turnLefts** are executed? How many **moves**? How many calls to **findMine**?

A good way to think about recursion and the recursive call is in terms of the specification of the instruction itself. In the preceding case, the specification is that when a robot executes this instruction it will walk a certain number of steps, say $k$, to a beeper, turn left, and then walk $k$ steps farther. Suppose we start the robot $N$ steps away from the beeper ($k = N$). In the instruction just presented, the ELSE clause has a **move** instruction first. That means that the robot is now $N - 1$ steps from the beeper. Therefore, by the specification, the recursive ($k = N - 1$) call will walk $N - 1$ steps forward, turn left, and then walk $N - 1$ steps beyond. We therefore need to supply one additional **move** instruction after the recursion to complete the required $N$ steps.

It will take solving a number of problems and a good deal of staring before recursion becomes as comfortable to use as iteration. A large part of this is because recursion requires some intuition to see the correct reduction, especially in difficult problems. This intuition will come with practice, which is just what the sample problems are designed to provide.

## 6.3  TAIL RECURSION AND LOOPING

Suppose we have an instruction with a WHILE loop and we would like to rewrite it so that it doesn't use a loop but still carries out the same task. To consider the simplest case, suppose that the outermost control mechanism in an instruction is a loop. For example, look at the instruction

```
void Beeper_Finder::findBeeper()
{
        while ( ! nextToABeeper())
        {
            move();
        }
}
```

By the definition of the WHILE given in Section 5.2, this is the same as

```
void Beeper_Finder::findBeeper()
{
    if ( ! nextToABeeper())
    {
        move();
        while ( ! nextToABeeper())   <--
        {                            <--
                move();              <-- findBeeper
        }                            <--
    }
}
```

However, the nested WHILE instruction in this latter form is exactly the body of **findBeeper** using the definition of **findBeeper** given first, so we can rewrite this second form as

```
void Beeper_Finder::findBeeper()
{
        if ( ! nextToABeeper())
        {
            move();
            findBeeper();
        }
}
```

Thus the first form, a WHILE, is equivalent to the last form, a recursive program. Also notice that we could just as easily transform the second form into the first because they are execution equivalent.

Notice, finally, that this is a special form of recursion, since after the recursive step (the nested **findBeeper**) there is nothing more to do in this instruction. It is, after all, the last instruction within an IF instruction, so when it is done, the IF is done, and therefore the instruction of which this is the body is done. This form of recursion is called <u>tail recursion</u>, because the recursive step comes at the very tail of the computation.

It is possible to prove formally that tail recursion is equivalent to WHILE looping. Therefore we can see that a WHILE loop is just a special form of recursion. So anything that you can do with a loop, you can also do with a recursive program. There are some deep and beautiful theories in computer science (and in mathematics) that have been developed from this observation.

By way of contrast, the `findMine` instruction discussed in Section 6.2 was certainly recursive, but it is not tail recursive, because the final `move` instruction follows the recursive message. That instruction is also equivalent to one using only WHILE loops, but, as suggested in Section 6.2, it is very convoluted.

## 6.4 GOING FORMAL

At the beginning of this chapter we saw that it is possible to get a robot to perform an operation repeatedly without using LOOP or WHILE instructions. Perhaps you are wondering whether there is a relationship between recursive programming and iterative programming. The answer, of course, is yes, and we would like to go a bit deeper into the relationship.

In Chapter 5 we learned about the WHILE instruction and how to use it. However, the description we gave of it was somewhat informal, relying on examples and intuition. That is fine at the beginning, but it is also useful to look at a formal definition of a WHILE statement, so that it can be analyzed logically.

Suppose we permit instructions themselves to be named. We don't permit this in the robot language itself, only in talking about the robot language. This is the so-called <u>meta level</u>, the level at which we don't use a thing (the programming language) but discuss and analyze it. In any case, suppose that we let the simple WHILE statement form "while (<test>){<instruction-list>}" be known as statement $W$. Let us also denote the <test> of the WHILE as $T$ and the <instruction-list> as $L$. Then $W$ can be written as

$W ==$ `while (` $T$ `){` $L$ `}`

The formal definition of $W$ is

$W ==$ `if (` $T$ `){` $L$ `;` $W$ `; }`

This says that to perform the WHILE instruction $W$ we must first test $T$ (if $(T)\ldots$) and if $T$ is false, do nothing at all, but if $T$ is true, then we must perform $L$ followed by $W$, the WHILE instruction itself. By the definition this means that we must test $T$ again, and if it is false do nothing else, but if it is true, we must perform $L$ again followed by $W$ again, and so on.

The looping should be clear from this description, but if you look at the definition we have written, you see the recursive nature of the WHILE. This means that the

WHILE statement *W* is defined in terms of itself, since *W* appears on the right side of the definition as well as the left. We hope that the *W* on the right is not exactly the same as the one on the left but a simpler, smaller version of the *W* that appears on the left. What that means is that for a WHILE loop to make sense or be defined, the execution of the instruction list *L* must partially solve the problem that the entire WHILE set out to solve and take us closer to termination of the loop. If that is not the case, and the execution of *L* leaves the robot in the same state, relative to termination, that it was in at the start, then the loop is guaranteed to run forever. This is because in this case the definition is purely circular and thus doesn't define anything.

## 6.5   SEARCHING

This section introduces two new instructions, **zigLeftUp** and **zagDownRight**, that move a robot diagonally northwest and southeast, respectively. Both of these instructions are defined by using only ur_Robot's instructions such as **turnLeft**, but we derive immense conceptual power from being able to think in terms of moving diagonally. For reasons that will become clear in the exercises, the class into which we put these instructions is **Mathematician**. It will have the class **Robot** as the parent class.

The following definitions introduce the stars of this section: **zigLeftUp** and **zagDownRight**. These direction pairs are not arbitrary; if a robot moves to the left and upward long enough, it eventually reaches the western boundary wall. The same argument holds for traveling down and toward the right, except that in this case the robot eventually reaches the southern boundary wall.

The other two possible direction pairs lack these useful properties: a robot will never find a boundary wall by traveling up and toward the right, and we cannot be sure which of the two boundary walls it will come upon first when traveling downward and to the left.

The following instructions define **zigLeftUp** and **zagDownRight**:

```
void Mathematician : zigLeftUp ()
{
                // Pre-condition:  facingWest and
                // frontIsClear
                // Post-condition:  facingWest
        move();
        turnRight();
        move();
        turnLeft();
}

void Mathematician :: zagDownRight()
{
                // Pre-condition:  facingSouth and
```

```
            // frontIsClear
            // Post-condition:  facingSouth
      move();
      turnLeft();
      move();
      turnRight();
}
```

Assume that we have a Mathematician named Karel. Observe that no part of these instructions forces Karel to move in the intended directions. To execute `zigLeftUp` correctly, Karel must be facing west; to execute `zagDownRight` correctly, Karel must be facing south. These requirements are the pre-conditions of the instructions. Recall that a pre-condition of an instruction is a condition that must be made true before a robot can correctly execute the instruction. We have seen many other examples of pre-conditions in this book.

For this example, the directional pre-condition of `zigLeftUp` is that Karel is facing west; likewise, the directional pre-condition of `zagDownRight` is that Karel is facing south. Karel's execution of these instructions, when their pre-conditions are satisfied, is shown in Figure 6-1.

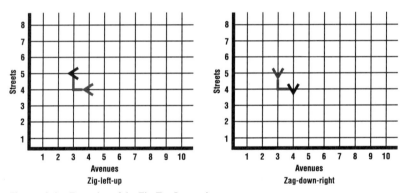

**Figure 6.1**  Execution of the Zig-Zag Instructions

Here is a statement that is loaded with terminology: the directional pre-conditions of `zigLeftUp` and `zagDownRight` are invariant over each instruction's execution. This just means that if Karel is facing west and it executes `zigLeftUp`, the robot is still facing west after the instruction has finished executing. This property allows Karel to execute a sequence of `zigLeftUp` instructions without having to reestablish their directional pre-condition. A similar statement holds about Karel's facing south and `zagDownRight`. Also observe that each instruction must be executed only when Karel's front is clear. This pre-condition is not invariant over the instructions, because Karel may be one block away from a corner where its front is blocked (for example, Karel may execute `zigLeftUp` while facing west on the corner of 4th Street and 2nd Avenue).

The first major instruction that we will write solves the problem of finding a beeper that can be located anywhere in the world. Our task is to write an instruction named **findBeeper** that positions Karel on the same corner as the beeper. We have seen a version of this problem in Chapter 5 in which both Karel and the beeper are in an enclosed room. This new formulation has less stringent restrictions: The beeper is placed on some arbitrary street corner in Karel's world, and there are no wall sections in the world. Of course, the boundary walls are always present.

One simple solution may spring to mind. In this attempt, Karel first goes to the origin and faces east. The robot then moves eastward on 1st Street looking for a beeper. If Karel finds a beeper on 1st Street, it has accomplished its task; if the beeper is not found on 1st Street, Karel moves back to the western wall, switches over to 2nd Street, and continues searching from there. Karel repeats this strategy until it finds the beeper. Unfortunately, a mistaken assumption is implicit in this search instruction: There is no way for Karel to know that the beeper is not on 1st Street. No matter how much of 1st Street Karel explores, the robot can never be sure that the beeper is not one block farther east.

It looks as if we and Karel are caught in an impossible trap, but there is an ingenious solution to our problem. As we might expect, it involves zig-zag moves. We need to program Karel to perform a radically different type of search pattern; Figure 6-2 shows such a pattern, and we use it here to define the **findBeeper** instruction.

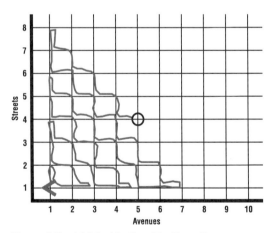

**Figure 6-2** A Method for Searching Every Corner

This search method expands the search frontier similar to the way water would expand over Karel's world from an overflowing sink at the origin. Roughly, we can view Karel as traveling back and forth diagonally on the fringe of this water wave. Convince yourself that this search pattern is guaranteed to find the beeper eventually, regardless of the beeper's location—in our analogy, we need to convince ourselves that the beeper will eventually get wet. We can use stepwise refinement to write the **findBeeper** instruction using this search method with the **zigLeftUp** and **zagDownRight** instructions:

```
void Mathematician :: findBeeper()
{
        goToOrigin();
        faceWest();
        while ( ! nextToABeeper() )
        {
            if ( facingWest() )
            {
                zigMove();
            }
            else
            {
                zagMove();
            }
        }
}
```

The **findBeeper** instruction starts by moving Karel to the origin and then facing west. (We saw how to write the **faceWest** instruction in Chapter 4.) These instructions establish the directional pre-condition for **zigLeftUp**. The WHILE loop's purpose is to keep Karel moving until it finds a beeper, and it is correct if the loop eventually terminates. The IF condition, which is nested within the body of the loop, determines which direction Karel has been traveling and continues moving the robot along the diagonal in this same direction. We continue the stepwise refinement by writing **zigMove** and **zagMove**.

```
void Mathematician :: zigMove()
{
            // Pre-condition: facingWest
        if ( frontIsClear() )
        {
            zigLeftUp ();
        }
        else
        {
            advanceToNextDiagonal();
        }
}
```

and

```
void Mathematician :: zagMove()
{
            // Pre-condition:  facingSouth()
        if ( frontIsClear() )
```

```
        {
                zagDownRight();
        }
        else
        {

                advanceToNextDiagonal();
        }
}
```

The moving instructions `zigMove` and `zagMove` operate similarly; therefore we discuss only `zigMove`. When Karel is able to keep zigging, the `zigMove` instruction moves it diagonally to the next corner. Otherwise, the robot is blocked by the western boundary wall and must advance northward to the next diagonal. We now write the instruction that advances Karel to the next diagonal.

```
    void Mathematician :: advanceToNextDiagonal()
    {
            if ( facingWest() )
            {
                    faceNorth();
            }
            else
            {
                    faceEast();
            }
            move();
            turnAround();
    }
```

The **advanceToNextDiagonal** instruction starts by facing Karel away from the origin; it turns a different direction depending on whether the robot has been zigging or zagging. In either case, Karel then moves one corner farther away from the origin and turns around. If Karel has been zigging on the current diagonal, after executing **advanceToNextDiagonal**, the robot is positioned to continue by zagging on the next diagonal, and vice versa.

Observe that when Karel executes a **zigLeftUp** or a **zagDownRight** instruction, it must visit two corners; the first is visited temporarily and the second is on a diagonal from Karel's starting corner. When thinking about these instructions, we should ignore the intermediate corner and just remember that these instructions move Karel diagonally. Also notice that the temporarily visited corner is guaranteed not to have a beeper on it, because it is part of the wave front that Karel visited while it was on the previous diagonal sweep.

Trace Karel's execution of **findBeeper** in the sample situation presented in Figure 6-2 to acquaint yourself with its operation. Try to get a feel for how all these instructions fit together to accomplish the task. Pay particularly close attention to the `advanceToNextDiagonal` instruction. Test **findBeeper** in the situation where the beeper is on the origin and in situations where the beeper is next to either boundary wall.

## 6.6  DOING ARITHMETIC

One of the things that computers do well is manipulating numbers. Robots can be taught to do arithmetic, as we shall see. One way to represent numbers in the robot world is to use beepers. We could represent the number 32 by putting 32 beepers on a corner, but we can be more sophisticated. Suppose that we represent the different digits of a multidigit number separately. Therefore, to represent the number 5132, we could using 2nd street as an example of a place to put the number, put five beepers at 2nd Street and 1st Avenue, one beeper at 2nd and 2nd, three beepers at 2nd and 3rd, and two beepers at 2nd and 4th. We could write a whole column of numbers as shown in Figure 6-3.

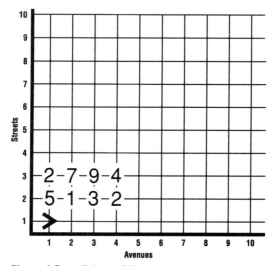

**Figure 6-3**    A Column of Numbers to be Added

Let's start with a simpler case, however, and just add up a column of single-digit numbers. See Figure 6–4 for an example. Suppose we start with an **Adder** robot on 1st Street with a column of numbers represented by beepers north of it. On each such corner there will be between one and nine beepers. We want to "write' on 1st Street the decimal number representing the sum of the column. Since we must "carry" if the total number of beepers is more than 9, we assume that we are not starting at 1st Avenue.

Our adder robot will utilize two helper robots. The first of these will check to see if a carry is necessary, and the second will actually do the carry if it is necessary. Since

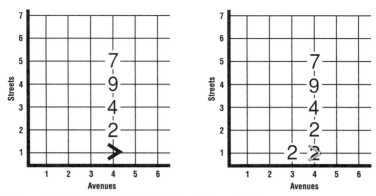

**Figure 6-4**    Adding Single-Digit Numbers Before and After

these robots will need to be created and find the adder robot that created them, we will start with a base class that provides this finding instruction. All of our other classes for this problem will be derived as subclasses of this base class, **Finder**. We won't actually create any Finder robots, however. This class is just a convenient place to place instructions that must be common to other classes.

```
class Finder: Robot
{
        void turnAround();
        void turnRight();
        void moveToRobot();
};

void Finder :: moveToRobot() // Robot directly ahead.
{
        while( ! nextToARobot() )
        {
            move();
        }
}

class Carrier: Finder
{
        void carryOne(); // Carry a ''one'' to
                         // the next column
};

class Checker: Finder
{
        Boolean enoughToCarry(); // Are there
                                 // enough to
```

```
                                        //   require
                                        //   carrying?
                    . . .
};

class Adder: Finder // Always create on 1st
                    // Street, facing north.
{
        Carrier Carry(1,1, East, infinity);
        Checker Check(1,1, East, 0);
        void gatherHelpers();
        void addColumn();
                    . . .
};

void Adder :: gatherHelpers()

{
        Carry.findRobot();
        Carry.turnLeft();
        Check.findRobot();
        Check.turnLeft();
}
```

Once the adder robot has created its helpers, it can execute **addColumn**. To do this it merely picks up all of the beepers north of it until it finds an empty corner, returns to 1st Street, deposits all of the beepers there, and then has the helpers finish the task.

```
void Adder :: addColumn() // Facing north on 1st
                         // Street.
{
        move();
        while(nextToABeeper()
        {
            pickBeeper();
            if ( ! nextToABeeper() )
            {
                    move();
            }
        }
        turnAround();
        while( frontIsClear() )
        {
            move();
        }
```

```
        turnAround();
        while ( anyBeepersInBeeperBag()   )
        {
             putBeeper();
        }
        // Compute the quotient and the remainder.
        while( Check.enoughToCarry()
        {
             Carry.carryOne();
        }
   }
```

Carrying is quite simple. Notice that we gave the **Carrier** an infinite number of beepers in its beeper-bag, so it can't possibly run out.

```
   void Carrier :: carryOne() // Facing north on 1st
                              // Street.
   {
        turnLeft();
        move();   // Note: Error shutoff  here if
                  // we try to carry
                  // from 1st Street.
        putBeeper;
        turnAround();
        move();
        turnLeft();
   }
```

The Checker robot does all of the interesting work. It must determine whether there are 10 or more beepers on the current corner. If there are it must return true, otherwise false. It can try to pick up10 beepers to check this. However, it has more to do, since it is going to be called repeatedly to see how many multiples of 10 there really are. Therefore it must find a way to dispose of each group of 10 beepers before it attempts to check for the next group of 10. It has another important task also. If it finds fewer than 10 beepers in a group, it must leave them on the current corner. This is to account for the first digit of the answer, the one that isn't carried.

```
   Boolean Checker :: enoughToCarry() // Facing north
                                      // on 1st Street.
   {
             loop(10)
             {
                 if (nextToABeeper() )
                 {
                      pickBeeper();
                 }
```

```
            else
            {
                    emptyBag();
                    return false;
            }
    }
    // We have found 10 beepers.
    move();
    emptyBag(); // leave them on 2nd Street.
    turnAround();
    move();
    turnAround();
    return true;
}
```

To finish we need only add **emptyBag** to the **Checker** class:

```
void Checker :: emptyBag()
{
        while( anyBeepersInBeeperBag() )
        {
                putBeeper();
        }
}
```

Now we are ready to tackle the problem of a multicolumn sum. Notice that if we start at the right end of the row of values and just slide the adder and its helpers to the left after adding a column, the three robots will be positioned for the next column. Then, working from right to left, we will compute the correct sum since we carry into a column before that column is added.

We need two additional instructions in the **Adder** class: **slideLeft** and **addAll**. Instruction **slideLeft** is easy:

```
void Adder :: slideLeft()
{

        turnLeft();
        move();
        turnRight();
        carrier.turnLeft();
        carrier.move();
        carrier.turnRight();
        checker.turnLeft();
        checker.move();
        checker.turnRight();
}
```

How will **addAll** know when it is done adding columns? One way is to have the leftmost number start on 2nd Avenue so that there is room to carry any value from the leftmost column. The Adder will then need to check to see whether it is on 2nd Avenue before adding. This requires a new predicate:

```
Boolean Adder :: onSecondAve()     //Precondition:
                                   //facing north and
                                   //not on  1st Avenue.
{
      turnLeft();
      move();
      if (frontIsClear)
      {
            turnAround();
            move();
            turnLeft();
            return false;
      }
      turnAround();
      move();
      turnLeft();
      return true;
```

We are now ready to write the **addAll** instruction.

```
void Adder :: addAll()
{
        while( ! onSecondAve() )
        {
            addColumn();
            slideLeft();
        }
        addColumn();
}
```

## 6.7  POLYMORPHISM—WHY WRITE MANY PROGRAMS WHEN ONE WILL DO?

Polymorphism means literally "many forms." In object-oriented programming it refers to the fact that messages sent to objects (robots) may be interpreted differently depending on the class of the object (robot) receiving the message. Perhaps the best way to think of this is to remember that a robot is autonomous in its world. We send it messages and it responds. It doesn't come with a remote control unit by which the user directs its actions. Rather, it "hears" the messages sent to it and responds according to its internal dictionary. Recall that each robot consults its own internal dictionary of instructions to select the instruction that it uses to respond to any message. The new version of any instruction, then, changes the meaning of the instruction for robots of the new class.

To illustrate the consequences of this, let's take a somewhat dramatic, though not very useful, example. Suppose we have the following two classes:

```
class Putter: Robot
{
        void move();
};

class Getter: Robot
{
        void move();
};
```

Both classes override the **move** instruction and nothing more. Suppose the implementations of these two instructions are as follows:

```
void Putter::move()
{
        Robot:: move();
        if (anyBeepersInBeeperBag())
        {
               putBeeper();
        }
}

void Getter::move()
{
        Robot :: move();
        while (nextToABeeper())
        {
               pickBeeper();
        }
}
```

Thus a **Putter** robot puts beepers on corners that it moves to and **Getter** robots sweep corners to which they move. Suppose now that we use these two classes in the following task:

```
task
{        Putter Lisa(1, 1, East, 100);
```

```
Getter Tony(2, 1, East, 0);

loop (10)
{
        Lisa.move();
}
loop (10)
{
        Tony.move();
}
}
```

If the world contains a beeper on each of the first 10 corners of 1st Street and also each of the first 10 corners of 2nd Street, then when the task is done, there will be two beepers on each of the first 10 blocks of 1st Street and none on the corresponding blocks of 2nd Street. There is nothing surprising about this, but note that both Lisa and Tony responded to the same messages in identical (relative) situations.

The meaning of polymorphism is even deeper than this, however. In fact, the names that we use to refer to robots are not "burned in" to the robots themselves, but only a convenience for the user. A given robot can be referred to by different names, called aliases. In order to use aliases we need to introduce some additional features of the robot programming language.

First, we declare that a name will be used as an alias by marking it with an asterisk:

```
Robot *Karel; // "Karel" will refer to some robot
              // indirectly.
```

Secondly, we need to "assign" a value to the name *Karel.* In other words we need to specify which robot the name *Karel* will refer to. We do this with an assignment instruction:

```
Karel = &Tony;
```

This establishes Karel as an alternative name (alias) for the robot also known as Tony. We could just as easily make the name *Karel* refer to the robot Lisa. It is very important to note, however, that an alias doesn't refer to any robot until we assign a value to the name.

We also use a slightly different syntax when sending a message to a robot referred to by an alias. This is to emphasize that we are using an alias. The notation uses the symbol -> instead of the dot.

```
Karel -> turnLeft();
```

will send the **turnLeft** message to the robot referred to by the name *Karel.*

Suppose now that we consider the slightly revised task that follows. We use the same setup and assume that the world is as before. The only difference is that we refer to the robots using the name *Karel* in each case.

```
task
{        Robot *Karel;
         Putter Lisa(1, 1, East, 100);
         Getter Tony(2, 1, East, 0);

         Karel = &Lisa;        // ''Karel'' refers
                               // to Lisa;

         loop (10)
         {
             Karel->move();  // Lisa puts down 10
                             // beepers

         }
         Karel = &Tony;        // ''Karel'' refers to
                               // Tony

         loop (10)

         {
             Karel->move();  // Tony sweeps 10
                             // blocks

         }
}
```

So note that not only can we have identical messages (**move**) referring to different actions, but even if the message statements as a whole are identical that is, (**Karel->move();**) we can have different actions. Notice, though, that we are still sending messages to two different robots, and that these robots are from different classes. It is even possible to arrange it so that different things happen on two different executions of the same statement. Consider the following:

```
task
{        Robot *Karel;
         Putter Lisa(1, 1, East, 100);
         Getter Tony(2, 1, East, 0);

         loop (10)
         {
             Karel = &Lisa;              // ''Karel''
                                         // refers to
                                         // Lisa;
             loop (2)
```

```
            {
                    Karel->move();     // ??
                    Karel = &Tony;     // ''Karel''
                                       // refers to
                                       // Tony


            }
        }
    }
```

Note that the **move** message is sent 20 times, but 10 times it is sent to Lisa and 10 times to Tony, alternately. Again, 1st Street gets extra beepers and 2nd Street gets swept.

## 6.8   CONCLUSION

Finally, we want to ask the question: When is it appropriate to design a new class, and when should we modify or add to an existing robot class?

The full answer to this question is beyond the scope of this book, because there are many things to be considered in this decision, but we can set some general guidelines here. If, in your judgment, a robot class contains errors or omissions, by all means modify it. Here omissions mean that there is some instruction (action or predicate) that is needed to complete the basic functionality of the class or to make robots in the class do what the class was designed to do.

On the other hand, if we have a useful class, and we need additional functionality, especially more specialized functionality than that provided by the class we already have, then building a new class as a subclass of the given one is appropriate. This way, when we need a robot with the original capabilities, we can use the original class, and when we need the new functionality we can use the new one. Sometimes the choice is made because we find that most of the instructions of some class are exactly what we want, but one or two instructions would serve better in the new problem if they were modified or extended.

## 6.9   HIERARCHY OF KNOWN CLASSES

Figure 6-5 gives the relationships between the various classes that we have discussed in this book. We omit the classes discussed only in the exercises. You should complete the figure with the classes you have built. Notice that the structure of the diagram is a tree, with ur_Robot as the root. As we move away from the root, we find derived classes (descendant classes). As we move toward the root we find parent and ancestor classes.

Notice that the farther we are from the root of this tree, the more specialized the robots become. This means that they are more adapted to specific tasks, but it can also mean that they are less useful generally. For example, a Sweeper robot is not especially efficient in a world without beepers, and just plain useless in a world in which the beepers serve as landmarks but are not to be disturbed.

```
ur_Robot
        Mile_Walker
        Mile_Mover
        Stair_Sweeper
        Big_Stepper
        Harvester
        Field_Harvester
        Long_Harvester
        Choreographer
        Contractor
        Mason
        Roofer
        Carpenter
        Robot
                Checker_Robot
                Harvester
                        Sparse_Harvester
                Prospector
                Racer
                Replanter
                Beeper_Finder
                Beeper_Controller
                Beeper_Sweeper
                Guard
                Sweeper
                Mathematician
                Finder
                Checker
                Carrier
                Adder
                Putter
                Getter
```

**Figure 6-5**  The Hierarchy of Classes

## 6.10  PROBLEM SET

The following problems use the recursion, searching, and arithmetic instructions discussed in this chapter. Some of the following problems use combinations of the **zigLeftUp** and **zagDownRight** instructions, or simple variants of these. Each problem is difficult to solve, but once a plan is discovered (probably through an "aha experience"), the program that implements the solution will not be too difficult to write. You may also assume that there are no wall sections in the world. Finally, you should assume that our robot, Karel, starts with no beepers in its beeper-bag unless you are told otherwise. Do not make any assumptions about Karel's starting corner or starting direction unless they are specified in the problem.

1. Rewrite your program that solves Problem 21 in Section 5.9 using a recursive instruction instead of an iterative one.

2. Karel has graduated to advanced carpet layer. Karel must carpet the completely enclosed room. Only one beeper can be placed on each corner. The room may be any size and any shape. Figure 6–6 shows one possible floor plan. The gray area is not to be carpeted by Karel. Karel may start from any place within the room and may be facing any direction.

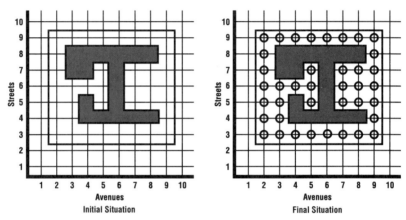

**Figure 6-6**  A Big Carpeting Job

3. Rewrite both `zigLeftUp` and `zagDownRight` so that they automatically satisfy their directional pre-conditions.

4. Assume that there is a beeper on 1st Street and *N*th Avenue. Program Karel to find it and move to *N*th Street and 1st Avenue.

5. Assume that there is a beeper on *S*th Street and *A*th Avenue, and that Karel has two beepers in its beeper-bag. Program Karel to put the beepers from its beeper-bag onto 1st Street and *A*th Avenue and *S*th Street and 1st Avenue. The original beeper must remain at the corner on which it starts.

6. Assume that there is a beeper on 1st Street and *A*th Avenue. Program Karel to double the avenue number; the robot must move this beeper to 1st Street and 2*A*th Avenue. (For example, a beeper on 1st Street and 7th Avenue must be moved to 1st Street and 14th Avenue.) *Hint:* Use the west boundary wall as in Problem 4.

7. Assume that Karel starts its task with an infinite number of beepers in its beeper-bag. Also assume that there is a beeper on 1st Street and *N*th Avenue. Program Karel to leave *N* beepers on the origin.

**8.** Assume that there is a beeper on Sth Street and 1st Avenue and a beeper on 1st Street and Ath Avenue. Program Karel to put one of these beepers on Sth Street and Ath Avenue. Karel must put the other beeper in its beeper-bag. *Hint:* There are many ways to plan this task. Here are two suggestions: (1) Move one beeper south while moving the other beeper north; (2) continue moving one beeper until it is directly over (or to the right of) the stationary beeper. If done correctly, both methods will result in one beeper being placed on the answer corner.

**9.** Assume that there is a beeper on Ath Street and Bth Avenue. Program a Mathematician robot to find the beeper, pick it up, and transport it to 1st Street and $(A + B)$th Avenue. *Hint.* When you find the beeper, the sum of your street and avenue numbers will be $A + B$. If you move south one block and also east one block, the sum will still be the same, since your street number will have decreased by one and your avenue number will have increased by one.

**10.** Assume that Karel has a beeper in its beeper-bag and that there is another beeper on 1st Street and Ath Avenue. Program Karel to place one of the beepers on 1st Street and $(2^A)$th Avenue. This expression is 2 raised to the Ath power or 1 doubled A times. For example, when A is 5, $2^A$ is 32. *Hint:* This problem uses instructions similar to those used to solve Problem 6. Karel can use the second beeper to count the number of times it must double the number 1.

**11.** Repeat Problem 10, but this time the answer corner is 1st Street and $(3^A)$th Avenue. Try to reuse as much of the previous program as possible.

**12.** Program Karel to place beepers in an outward spiral until its beeper-bag is empty. Assume that Karel will run out of beepers before it is stopped by the boundary walls. One example is shown in Figure 6–7.

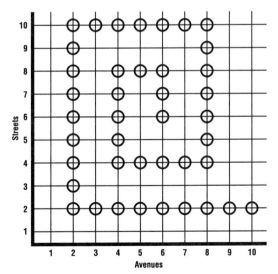

**Figure 6-7**  A Spiral

13. Assume that Karel has two beepers and that there is another beeper on $S$th Street and $A$th Avenue. Program Karel to deposit one of these beepers on the corner of 1st Street and $SA$th Avenue (this expression is $S$ multiplied by $A$).

14. Assume that Karel has three beepers in its beeper-bag and that there is another beeper on $S$th Street and $A$th Avenue. Program Karel to deposit a beeper on the corner of 1st Street and $(S^A)$th Avenue (this expression is $S$ raised to power of $A$).

15. Assume that Karel has three beepers in its beeper-bag and that there is another beeper on $S$th Street and $A$th Avenue. Program Karel to put a beeper on the corner of 1st Street and GCD($S,A$)th Ave. The GCD of two numbers is their greatest common divisor. For example, the GCD of 6 and 15 is 3. *Hint:* Use Euclid's subtractive instruction.

16. Assume that Karel has $N$ beepers in its beeper-bag. Program the robot to place beepers on 1st Street and all avenues that represent prime numbers between 1st Avenue and $(N - \sqrt{N})$th Avenue.

17. Program a robot named Karel to pick up a beeper at the west wall and return to the corner on which it starts. There may be other beepers in the path, but it is known that there is a beeper on 1st Avenue directly west of Karel's starting position. *Hint:* Think recursively.

18. Program a robot named Karel to pick up a beeper at the origin and return to the corner on which it starts. *Hint:* Think recursively.

19. Write a recursive program to solve Problem 25 in Section 5.9. *Hint:* If all of the piles of beepers were moved one block north, then 1st Street would be clear. The robot could then use two beepers to mark the beginning and ending avenues that it was supposed to sort. An overall plan could be to move the smallest pile between the two markers to the western marker avenue. That marker could then be moved one block east.

20. Write a recursive predicate to determine whether the number of beepers in a robot's beeper-bag is exactly the same as the number of beepers on the robot's current corner. You may assume that there is no wall immediately to the north of the robot.

21. Karel the Robot meets Carol the ur_Robot on a corner. How can Karel determine whether it has exactly the same number of beepers in its beeper-bag that Carol has? Each robot should finish with the same number of beepers that it starts with.

22. Karel and Carol again meet on a corner. Have them exchange beepers, so that Karel ends with the number of beepers Carol has initially and conversely. Assume that the corner they both occupy has no beepers.

23. Create a robot on each of the first 10 avenues of 1st Street. They each have zero or more beepers in their beeper-bag. Their task is to sort themselves in order of number of beepers, with the robot with the smallest number on 1st Avenue, and so on. Each robot can visit one of its neighbors and between

them decide which of their original corners each should occupy. Repetitions of this will sort the robots. When they are sorted, have each robot distribute its beepers along the streets of the avenue it occupies, one beeper per corner. The final picture should be similar to the final figure of Figure 5-31. Assume that there are no beepers in the world except the beepers carried by the robots.

**24.** What happens if we use an Adder robot to add the numbers 3102 and 4027? Devise a solution that covers this beyond-the-horizon situation.

**25.** Devise a solution to the problem we left unsolved in Chapter 5. Four robots are supposed to patrol a field of beepers, keeping equally spaced around the perimeter. You might try a solution with one leader and three helpers, as we did in the solution to the simpler problem. The leader will belong to a new class that you must design.

**26.** If you enjoy computer science and eventually take a course in computability theory, fondly recall the days you spent programming Karel and try to solve the following problem: Prove that Karel, even without the aid of any beepers, is equivalent to a Turing machine. *Hint:* Use the equivalence between Turing machines and 2-counter automata.

# APPENDIX A

# ROBOT PROGRAMMING SUMMARY

## PRIMITIVE INSTRUCTIONS

```
class ur_Robot

{       void move();            // A robot moves
                                // forward one block.
        void turnOff();         // A robot turns
                                // itself off.
        void turnLeft();        // A robot pivots
                                // 90 degrees left.
        void pickBeeper();      // A robot puts a
                                // beeper into its
                                // beeper-bag.
        void putBeeper();       // A robot puts a beeper
                                // on the corner.
};



class Robot: ur_Robot
{       Boolean frontIsClear();
        Boolean nextToABeeper();
        Boolean nextToARobot();
        Boolean facingNorth();
        Boolean facingSouth();
        Boolean facingEast();
        Boolean facingWest();
        Boolean anyBeepersInBeeperBag();
};
```

## CONDITIONAL INSTRUCTIONS

```
if (  <test>   )
{        <instruction>
         <instruction>
            .  .  .
         <instruction>
}

if (  <test>   )
{        <instruction>
         <instruction>
            .  .  .
         <instruction>
}
else
{        <instruction>
          <instruction>
            .  .  .
          <instruction>
}
```

## REPETITION INSTRUCTIONS

```
loop (  <positiveNumber>   )
{        <instruction>
         <instruction>
            .  .  .
         <instruction>
}

while (  <test>   )
{        <instruction>
         <instruction>
            .  .  .
         <instruction>
}
```

## MECHANISM FOR DECLARING NEW ROBOT CLASSES

```
class <newClassName>   :   <oldClassName>
{        <robotInitialization>                        // Local Robots
```

```
                <robotInitialization>
                . . .
                <robotInitialization>
                // New instructions.
                <returns> <newInstructionName> ( );
                <returns> <newInstructionName> ( );
                . . .
                <returns> <newInstructionName> ( );
        }
```

## MECHANISM FOR DEFINING NEW INSTRUCTIONS

```
        <returns><className>  ::   <instructionName>  ( )
        {       <instruction>
                <instruction>
                . . .
                <instruction>
        }
```

If <returns> is Boolean, then one or more of the <instructions> should be

**return** <BooleanValue>

## SPECIFYING A COMPLETE PROGRAM

```
        <includes>
        <newClassDefinitions>
        <newInstructionDefinitions>
        task
        {               <robotInitialization>
                        . . .
                        <robotInitialization>
                        <instruction>
                        <instruction>
                        . . .
                        <instruction>
        }
```

## BRACKETED WORDS

<...Name>   Any new word in letters, numbers, and "_" that
            begins with a letter

| | |
|---|---|
| \<BooleanValue\> | **true** or **false** |
| \<instruction\> | \<instructionName\>( ) **;** |
| | \<robotName\> **.** \<instructionName\>( ) **;** |
| | \<aliasName\> **->** \<instructionName\>( ) **;** |
| \<positiveNumber\> | Any positive integer |
| \<returns\> | **void** or **Boolean** |
| \<robotInitialization\> | |
| | \<className\> \<robotName\> |
| | (street, avenue, facing, beepers) **;** |
| \<test\> | \<BoolFunctionName\>( ) |
| | \<robotName\> **.** \<BoolFunctionName\>( ) |
| | \<aliasName\> **->**\<BoolFunctionName\>( ) |
| | **!** \<BoolFunctionName\>( ) |
| | **!** \<robotName\> **.** \<BoolFunctionName\>( ) |
| | **!** \<aliasName\> **->** \<BoolFunctionName\>( ) |

# APPENDIX B

# DIFFERENCES BETWEEN KAREL++ AND C++

The robot programming language was purposely made very similar to C++ because you might want to use Karel to help learn C++. There are some differences, however.

### task versus main

In Karel++ we name the main task block **task**. In C++ it is a function named *main*. This function is not a part of any class.

### Visibility of Class Features

In Karel++ local robots are assumed to be private to that robot, and new instructions and predicates are assumed to be public. C++ permits much more control over what is public and what is not.

### Robot Initializations

When a robot is local to a class, we have defined its initialization in the same way that we define initialization in the main task block. For example,

```
Mile_Walker Lisa(3, 2, East, 0);
```

In C++ such robots are initialized in special functions called *constructors* instead.

### Structured Statements: IF, WHILE, and LOOP

We required all such statements to include compound statements enclosed in { and }. C++ has no such limitation. It is possible in C++ to write

```
if (nextToABeeper())
    move();
```

where we require

```
if (nextToABeeper())
{ move();
}
```

This leads to a problem in C++ called the "dangling else problem," which will be discussed in any good C++ book.

## Other

In C++ our **Boolean** is spelled *bool.* Older C++ systems use *int.*

In C++ our **loop** instruction is replaced by a much richer instruction called *for.*

In C++ what we have called *aliases* are called *pointers.* Pointers have many additional capabilities.

In C++ what we have called *myself* is called *this.*

We have assumed that all Karel++ instructions and predicates are what C++ refers to as *virtual.* This is what enables polymorphism. C++ has additional options in this regard.

C++ would permit a class to inherit from several classes called *base classes,* and all classes in C++ need not derive from a common point such as ur_Robot.

# APPENDIX C

# DIFFERENCES BETWEEN KAREL++ AND JAVA

The robot programming language was purposely made very similar to Java since you might want to use Karel to help learn Java. There are some differences, however.

## task versus main

In Karel++ we name the main task block **task**. In Java it is a function named *main*. This function may be a part of any class.

## Visibility of Class Features

In Karel++ local robots are assumed to be private to that robot and new instructions and predicates are assumed to be public. Java permits much more control over what is public and what is not.

## Robot Initializations

In Java a robot initialization is the class name and robot name as here, but the rest is different. Robots are initialized by calling a built-in function named *new,* so a robot initialization would look like this:

```
Mile_Walker Lisa = new Mile_Walker(3, 2, East, 0);
```

instead of our

```
Mile_Walker Lisa(3, 2, East, 0);
```

## Polymorphism

In Java no special syntax is required to achieve polymorphism as discussed in Chapter 6. In fact, all robot names would be considered to be aliases in Java, and many names could be used to refer to the same robot.

## Structured Statements: IF, WHILE, and LOOP

We required all such statements to include compound statements enclosed in { and }. Java has no such limitation. It is possible in Java to write

```
if (nextToABeeper())
        move();
```

where we require

```
if (nextToABeeper())
{       move();
}
```

This leads to a problem in Java called the "dangling else problem," which will be discussed in any good Java book.

## Class Structure

In Java it is not possible to separate the instruction definitions from the class definition. In Java a class would look like the following (see the following text for the word *extends*):

```
class SomeRobot extends Robot
{       void doSomething()
        {       move();
                . . .
        }
        boolean testSomething()
        {       . . .
        }
}
```

## Other

In Java our **Boolean** is spelled *boolean.*
In Java our **loop** instruction is replaced by a much richer instruction called *for.*
In Java our **#include** would be *import,* although *import* is only approximately the same as *#include.*
In Java it would be possible to have many robots moving simultaneously.
In Java what we have called *myself* is called *this.*
In Java inheritance is indicated by the word *extends,* where we have used a colon.
In Java the semicolon after each class declaration is not required.

# Index of Terms, Classes, and Instructions